DISCARD

Cheers!

Cheers!

1,024 Toasts & Sentiments for Every Occasion

Kevin P. McDonald

BLACK DOG
& LEVENTHAL
PUBLISHERS
NEW YORK

Published by
Black Dog & Leventhal Publishers
151 West 19th Street
New York, NY 10011

Distributed by
Workman Publishing Company
708 Broadway
New York, NY 10003

Manufactured in the United States of America

Text by Kevin P. McDonald
Interior design by Cindy LaBreacht
Cover design by Filip Zawodnik

ISBN: 1-57912-358-9

Library of Congress Cataloging-in-Publication Data

Cheers! : 1,024 toasts & sentiments for every occasion /
[compiled by] Kevin P. McDonald.
    p. cm.
Includes index.
ISBN 1-57912-358-9
1. Toasts. I. McDonald, Kevin P. II. Title.

PN6341.C55 2004
808.5'1--dc22
                                    2004000013

g f e d c b a

Dedication

To my family and friends, who give

me so many reasons to toast them.

And to my wonderful editor,

Kylie Foxx, without whom this book

would still be just an idea.

Contents

How to Use This Book ix

The Perfect Delivery xiii
TOASTING DOS AND DON'TS

The Toasts—A to Z

How to Use This Book

Unless you are a seasoned motivational speaker or are otherwise used to addressing large groups of people, you may feel nervous about talking in front of a crowd, not to mention having to sound intelligent, witty, and warm, too. But your anxieties are completely natural and can be overcome if you are well prepared for the task at hand. This book will give you all the tools you need to pull off your toast like a pro; use it wisely, and it will give your words wings.

Flipping through the many toasts and quotes gathered in these pages, you may feel the urge to simply pick one that seems appropriate and then recite it. While running off a quick quote is a great way to raise glasses some of the time, there are certain occasions where you'll want the words to be more personal, and this book is an excellent resource for those times, too. Think of it as a springboard from which to create a toast that incorporates your experience, wit, and wisdom with meaningful quotes as well. If you take the time to really work out your thoughts and prepare your words, you'll find an endless stream of ideas and inspiration from the thousand or so quotes herein. Trust me, by the time you're done, you'll be a true toastmaster!

Searching the Sayings
(and Your Soul)

This book is divided into sections that correspond with some of the most common toasting occasions. While each quote has been placed under what seems to be its most logical heading, you'll find that many toasts can be used (or at least adapted) to fit a variety of situations.

As I mentioned earlier, some occasions may call for simply looking up a quote, copying it down, and reading it with your glass aloft. But other times creating a meaningful toast calls for a bit more work, and it's well worth it.

When you first begin to build your toast, go straight to the most obvious section for your occasion (so if you're preparing to laud a recent grad, go to the Graduation section) and pick out a couple of your favorite quotes. Once you're in the section, you'll notice that there's a brief introduction followed by a list of cross-references—I urge you to check out other sections until you find something that suits your needs. Finally, refer to the table of contents for any additional sections where an apropos quote might lurk.

Using the graduation speech as an example, after selecting some Graduation quotes you might turn to the Coming of Age section if you'd like to talk about how the graduate is getting older. Or you could search the New Beginnings section if you want to discuss the new path your grad is setting out on. By scouring these different topics, you'll be sure to find words that help express all you want to say, and that don't limit you to talking about the act of graduation itself.

Pulling It All Together

The most moving toasts are often personal accounts punctuated by well-chosen quotes. But don't become so bogged down in finding the perfect quote that you forget the most important part—personal experience. The key is striking a balance between anecdote and quote. Here are some general guidelines:

First: Sit down with a pen and paper and brainstorm some anecdotes about the subject of the toast. When you're done, sift through the stories and pick out a few that are either really funny or really telling, or hopefully both. But be careful—not all stories are appropriate for all occasions. The tale about your sloppy-drunk friend flashing old ladies might be great at a bachelor party but less than laughable in a toast to his new promotion. As always, use your best judgment.

Second: Think about what the stories you've chosen illustrate. Do they show the honoree's sensitive side? Do they talk about his or her unflagging loyalty or adventurous spirit? Try to find a theme that runs through each anecdote, and use it to guide your choice of quotes. The words you choose should complement the stories you're about to share, so that the whole toast is cohesive and has a logical flow.

Third: Pull it all together. You'll want to begin by introducing yourself and filling in a little background about how you know the person you're toasting. Then you might fold in a quote to set up your story; or you could regale your audience with an anecdote and sum it up with a quote. However you feel most comfortable organizing your toast is fine—just keep it short (under five minutes) and sweet, and it'll be swell!

Here's to You
(and that doesn't mean *you*)!

One of the challenges of toast writing is to inject personal anecdotes and experiences into the speech without injecting yourself. Keep in mind that although you're giving the toast, the toast is not about you! When you've completed your masterpiece, be sure to read it over. If you notice the words *I* and *me* every other sentence, you may need to do some serious slashing. You want the toast to be about the wonderful person you're honoring, about all the fantastic things he or she has done and plans to do. Even if you were present at (or responsible for!) lots of those fantastic things, bite your lip and, within reason, keep yourself out of it.

The Perfect Delivery
Toasting Dos and Don'ts

Tailoring Your Toast

This may sound obvious, but it's important to be mindful of your honoree and your audience when giving a toast. A good example of this is in the case of the best man at a wedding. It's possible that he'll have to deliver three or more different toasts to very different groups during the course of his career—for instance, at the bachelor party, rehearsal dinner, and wedding reception. While the bachelor-party toast should be irreverent (it's just the best man and the boys), the rehearsal-dinner toast should be more sentimental and intimate (since the audience is the couple's closest friends and relatives). And the wedding toast should be nearest in tone to the rehearsal-dinner toast but should assume less familiarity on the part of the audience, which will likely include some peripheral characters who won't know the honorees as well.

Tailoring a toast doesn't end with tweaking it to fit the audience. It can also mean changing the language of the quotes to suit the occasion. This may be necessary if you are combining ideas from different quotes, or if you choose a quote that expresses your feelings but sounds a little out of place. Imagine our best man again. He's found the perfect quote to quip at his best bud's Vegas bachelor party, but he might not feel comfortable delivering it in its original Old English. Instead he might prefer to translate the quote into his own vernacular, since he'll likely be dressed as Elvis and speaking to a crowd knee deep in tequila shooters.

Last but not least, make sure that when you do use a quote, you cite its author in some way. It's not quite fair to claim responsibility for someone else's beautiful turn of phrase, and if that doesn't deter you, there's always the risk of exposure. Think of our poor best man—he delivers a lovely line by the Bard only to be exposed by the exotic dancer who "daylights" as a Shakespearean scholar. Hey, you never know!

The Two Rs—Write It Down, but Don't Read It

Look, if you're going to read your toast from a piece of paper, you might as well just print out enough copies for everyone and let them read it on their own time. It's not a bedtime story, it's a toast. You need to prepare well enough that you don't have to read it. While it's a very good idea to write out your toast* beforehand, you don't want to read it for the first time at the event or you'll wind up reciting it like a sixth-grade book report. To avoid this dangerous pitfall, it's a good idea to read your

---

*Tip: Save whatever you write down—a copy of the full toast can make a very meaningful gift for the honoree.

toast aloud a bunch of times before you "perform" it—you'll become familiar with the content and cadence of the writing, and you'll more or less start to commit it to memory.

This is not to say, however, that you should memorize the whole toast outright. Speaking from memory can get very tricky if you forget a key word or skip over an important sentiment, and you don't want to end up calling "line!" to the unlucky soul who's holding your cue card. It's perfectly acceptable to use a few mnemonic aids—after all, it's a toast, not a test! If you'd like to have the words in front of you, you might consider jotting down an outline and the most significant elements on an index card. These talking points, rather than the full speech, will help jostle your memory but will prevent you from reciting the toast like a liturgy. Plus, an index card transfers discreetly from purse or suit pocket to the palm of your hand. Or if you'd prefer to have some portion mastered, you could memorize the quotes and keep notes of your own words, or vice versa. Everybody is different when it comes to preparation and memorization, so use whatever method seems best for you.

Last but Not Least, Keep It Short and Sweet

Think of it this way: No one comes to an event just to hear a toast, so you don't want to make it seem like the toast is the main event. Your job is to add a little poignancy to the occasion. You are giving people a chance to stop and think about the importance of whatever occasion you are toasting to. The best toasts are five minutes or less, so keep your tongue from wagging too much and you should do very well.

So now that you've got the basics down, get toasting . . . Good luck and bottoms up!

The Toasts

A to Z

Achievement

Congratulations! Next time one of your friends wins the Nobel Prize, or the prize at the bottom of a Cracker Jack box, you'll have words commensurate with such a grand achievement (sometimes just getting through the day is achievement enough for a toast, don't you think?). No matter the cause for celebration, when you get to ching-chinging it's nice have something to say besides, "Congrats, dude" (although that's pretty good, too).

See also: Coming of Age, page 55, Graduation, page 105, and Promotions, page 181.

* * *

Let each become all that he was created capable of becoming.
                                    —Thomas Carlyle

The reward of a thing well done is to have done it.

—Ralph Waldo Emerson

* * *

It is not by spectacular achievements that man can be transformed, but by will.

—Henrik Ibsen

* * *

The heights by great men reached and kept
Were not attained by sudden flight,
But they, while their companions slept,
Were toiling upward in the night.

—Henry Wadsworth Longfellow

* * *

God gives nothing to those who keep their arms crossed.

(West African proverb)

* * *

People today distinguish between knowledge and action and pursue them separately, believing that one must know before he can act. . . . They say [they will wait] till they truly know before putting their knowledge into practice. Consequently, to the end of their lives, they will never act and also will never know.

—Wang Yang-ming

* * *

You can do anything in this world if you are prepared to take the consequences.

—W. Somerset Maugham

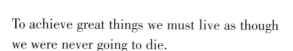

To achieve great things we must live as though we were never going to die.

—Luc de Clapiers, marquis de Vauvenargues

Deliberation is the work of many men. Action, of one alone.

—Charles de Gaulle

What we learn to do we learn by doing.

—Aristotle

* * *

The merit of action lies in finishing it to the end.

—Genghis Khan

Bachelors & Bachelorettes

A much-maligned yet more often envied
state of being, bachelorhood straddles
the fence between blessing and curse.
Sure, you can drink milk straight from
the carton at 3 A.M., but there's no one
there to wipe your milk mustache.
Whether you're bemoaning folks' loss
of freedom or welcoming them back to it,
the following toasts should give you a hand.

*See also: Drinking, page 59, Friendship,
page 85, Husbands & Wives, page 125,
and Weddings & Anniversaries, page 197.*

✳ ✳ ✳

Here's to marriage—the last decision you'll be
allowed to make.

7

When I said I should die a bachelor,
I did not think I should live till I were married.

—William Shakespeare

The best works, and of greatest merit for the
public, have proceeded from the unmarried or
childless.

—Francis Bacon

Misses! The tale that I relate
This lesson seems to carry
Choose not alone a proper mate,
But proper time to marry.

—William Cowper

A man who desires to get married should know
either everything or nothing.

—Oscar Wilde

Marriage is either kill or cure.

May the single be married—and the married
happy.

Marriage is a lottery in which men stake their
liberty, and women their happiness.

—Madame de Rieux

I should like to know the proper function of
women, if it is not to make reasons for husbands
to stay at home, and still stronger reasons for
bachelors to go out.

—George Eliot

A good dog, a good book, a good wife, perhaps.
But in all events, may your life be long and your
pipe sweet.

Here's to living single and drinking double.

An unwilling woman given to a man in marriage
is not his wife but his enemy.

—Plautus

A young man married is a man that's marr'd.

—William Shakespeare

He that hath a wife and children hath given
hostages to fortune; for they are impediments to
great enterprises, either of virtue or mischief.

—Francis Bacon

Nothing is more distasteful than that entire
complacency and satisfaction which beam in
the countenances of a new-married couple.

—Charles Lamb

Marriage has many pains, but celibacy has no pleasures.

Nobody knows how to manage a wife but a bachelor.

—George Coleman the Elder

I would advise no man to marry who is not likely to propagate understanding.

—Samuel Johnson

Love is the story of a woman's life, but only an episode in the life of a man.

—Germaine Necker, baronne de Staël-Holstein

Bachelor—A selfish, callous, undeserving man who has cheated some poor woman out of a divorce.

Bachelor—A man who never makes the same mistake once.

Never trust a husband too far, nor a bachelor too near.

—Helen Rowland

Here's to being single,
Drinking doubles,
and seeing triple!

It is a truth universally acknowledged, that
a single man in possession of a good fortune,
must be in want of a wife.
—Jane Austen

Bachelor's fare, bread and cheese, and kisses.

—Jonathan Swift

Champagne Sorbet Punch

Champagne or sparkling wine (2 bottles)
White dessert wine (1 bottle)
Lemon sorbet* (1 quart)

Combine champagne and wine in a punch
bowl and stir gently. Just before serving,
add a block of ice and scoops of the sorbet.

*Other fruit-flavored sorbets can be substituted.

Serves 15-20

Birthdays

Toastmaster, beware! A birthday is a love 'em or hate 'em occasion, one that can be very touchy for some people. When you are honoring the birthday boy or girl, make sure that his or her glass is raised for the toast—not as a weapon. Remind your toastee that along with hairy ears, impaired vision, and loss of memory, with age comes wisdom. And if nothing else, you can drink to that!

 See also: Coming of Age, page 55.

I am thankful to old age, which has increased my avidity for conversation, while it has removed that for eating and drinking.

—Cicero

Life well spent is long.

—Leonardo da Vinci

Here's a toast to the future;
A sigh for the past;
We can love and remember,
And hope to the last,
And for all the base lies,
That the Almanacs hold
While there's love in the heart,
We can never grow old.

As soon as people are old enough to know better,
they don't know anything at all.

—Oscar Wilde

Be wise with speed,
A fool at forty is a fool indeed.

—Edward Young

Verily, to honor an old man is showing respect
to God.

—Muhammad

Wherever your life ends, it is all there. The
advantage of living is not to be measured by
length, but by use; some men have lived long,
and lived little; attend to it while you are in it. It
lies in your will, not in the number of years, for
you to have lived enough.

—Michel Eyquem de Montaigne

A lad of a "certain age," which means
Certainly aged.

—George Gordon, Lord Byron

To the old guard, the older we grow,
The more we take and the less we know.
At least the young men tell us so,
But the day will come, when they shall know
Exactly how far a glass can go,
To win the battle, 'gainst age, the foe.
Here's youth . . . in a glass of wine.

—James Monroe McLean

Old age isn't so bad when you consider
the alternatives.

—Maurice Chevalier

Gather ye rose-buds while ye may,
Old Time still a flying;
And the same flower that blooms today,
Tomorrow may be dying.

—Robert Herrick

Live as long as you please, you will strike
nothing off the time you will have to spend dead.

—Michel Eyquem de Montaigne

Nobody loves life like an old man.

—Sophocles

Time and tide wait for no man—but time always
stands still for a woman of thirty.

—Robert Frost

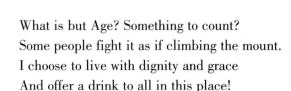

What is but Age? Something to count?
Some people fight it as if climbing the mount.
I choose to live with dignity and grace
And offer a drink to all in this place!

Old men are fond of giving good advice, to console themselves for being no longer in a position to give bad examples.

—François, duc de la Rochefoucauld

Time carries all things, even wits, away.

—Virgil

Few people know how to be old.

—François, duc de la Rochefoucauld

The old believe everything: the middle-aged suspect everything: the young know everything.

—Oscar Wilde

The old forget, the young don't know.

No wise man ever wished to be younger.

—Jonathan Swift

Middle Age—When a man says he is going to begin saving next month.

May you die in bed at ninety-five years,
Shot by a jealous wife!

As long as a woman can look ten years younger than her own daughter she is perfectly satisfied.

—Oscar Wilde

May you live as long as you like and have all you like as long as you live.

Whenever a man's friends begin to compliment him about looking young, he may be sure that they think he is growing old.

—Washington Irving

May the Lord love us but not call us too soon.

* * *

Let's drink—while we still can.

* * *

Enjoy the Spring of Love and Youth,
To some good Angel leave the rest,
The time will teach you soon enough
There are no birds in the last year's nest.

—Robert Herrick

Here's to your health! You make Age curious,
Time furious, and all of us envious!

Here's to you! No matter how old you are, you
don't look it!

May you live as long as you want and never want
as long as you live.

A graceful and honorable old age is the
childhood of immortality.

—Pindar

May you enter heaven late.

Age is something to brag about in the wine cellar
and forget about on your birthday.

Ad multo annos! (To many years!)

Many happy returns of the day of your birth:
Many blessings to brighten your pathway on earth;
Many friendships to cheer and provoke you to
    mirth;
Many feastings and frolics to add to your girth.

We grow neither better nor worse as we get old,
but more like ourselves.

The young man who has not wept is a savage, and
the old man who will not laugh is a fool.

—George Santayana

Birthdays are good for you. The more of them you
have, the longer you live.

If only youth knew, if only old age could.

—Henri Estienne

Here's to your good health, and your family's good
health, and may you all live long and prosper.

—Washington Irving

I wish thee health,
I wish thee wealth,
I wish thee gold in store,
I wish thee heaven upon earth
What could I wish thee more?

* * *

At twenty years of age, the will reigns; at thirty,
the wit; and at forty, the judgment.

—Benjamin Franklin

A toast to your coffin.

May it be of hundred-year-old oak.

And may we plant the tree together tomorrow.

* * *

To keep the heart unwrinkled, to be hopeful,
kindly, cheerful, reverent, that is to triumph over
old age.

—Thomas B. Aldrich

* * *

Age does not make us childish, as some say; it
finds us true children.

—Johann Wolfgang von Goethe

* * *

Happy birthday to you,
and many to be,
with friends who are true
as you are to me.

* * *

Let us take care that age does not make more
wrinkles on our spirit than on our face.

—Michel Eyquem de Montaigne

* * *

Fill to him, to the brim,
Round the table let it roll.
The divine says the wine
Cheers the body and the soul.

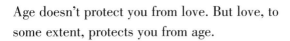

Age doesn't protect you from love. But love, to some extent, protects you from age.

—Jeanne Moreau

Youth knows no age.

—Pablo Picasso

The young have aspirations that never come to pass, the old have reminiscences of what never happened. It's only the middle-aged who are really conscious of their limitations.

—Saki

May your glasses always be full,
May the roof over your head always be strong,
And may you be in heaven half an hour before the devil knows you're dead.

May you live to be a hundred—with one extra year to repent.

No matter how old you are—you don't look it!

When I was young, I was told: 'You'll see, when you're fifty.' I'm fifty and I haven't seen a thing.

—Erik Satie

Another candle on your cake?
Why, that's no cause to pout.
Be grateful that you have the strength
To blow the damn thing out!

Do not resist growing old. Many are denied the
privilege.

May we all be together to toast your hundredth
birthday.

Age will not be defied.

—Francis Bacon

Here's to health in homely rhyme
To our oldest classmate, Father Time;
May our last survivor live to be
As bold and wise and as thorough as he!

—Oliver Wendell Holmes

Here's to you on your day of days.
We lift our glasses and sing your praise.

Here's to you on your day of days,
And all the whole year through,
For the best that life can give you
Is none too good for you.

May you live all the days of your life.

* * *

What though youth gave love and rose,
Age still leaves us friends and wine.

—Thomas Moore

* * *

My heart leaps up when I behold
A rainbow in the sky:
So was it when my life began;
So is it now I am a man;
So be it when I shall grow old,
Or let me die!

—William Wordsworth

* * *

To you on your birthday—
Now tell us the truth—
Where did you find
The fountain of youth?

* * *

Don't worry about the future,
The present is all thou hast,
The future will soon be present,
And the present will soon be past.

* * *

What youth deemed crystal, Age finds out was
dew.

—Robert Browning

May the most you wish for
Be the least you get.

May you be merry and lack nothing.

—William Shakespeare

Forget about the past, you can't change it.
Forget about the future, you can't predict it.
Forget about the present, I didn't get you one.

Avenge yourself: Live long enough to be
a problem to your children.

Youth is a blunder; Manhood a struggle;
Old Age a regret.

—Benjamin Disraeli

* * *

Birthdays were never like this when I had 'em.

* * *

The only time you really live fully is from thirty
to sixty. The young are slaves to dreams; the old,
servants of regrets. Only the middle-aged have all
their five senses in the keeping of their wits.

—Hervey Allen

* * *

To your birthday, glasses held high,
Glad it's you who's older—not I.

I wish you healthy, I wish you well,
and happiness galore.
I wish you luck for you and friends;
what could I wish you more?
May your joys be as deep as the oceans,
your troubles as light as its foam.
And may you find sweet peace of mind,
wherever you may roam.

Man arrives as a novice at each age of his life.

—Nicholas Chamfort

May thy life be long and happy,
Thy cares and sorrows few;
And the many friends around thee
Prove faithful, fond, and true.
Happy are we met, happy have we been,
Happy may we part, and happy meet again.

Age is something that doesn't matter, unless you
are a cheese.

—Billie Burke

It's not the years in your life that count—it's the
life in your years.

You're never too old to become younger.

—Mae West

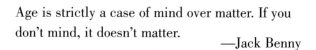

Age is strictly a case of mind over matter. If you don't mind, it doesn't matter.

—Jack Benny

Young men think old men fools; but old men know young men are fools.

—George Chapman

To Age! To Age! Why does one care?
As the wrinkles grow longer and gray graces
   your hair.
Life should be simple because when push comes
   to shove,
The only one counting is the good Lord above!

You're not too old when your hair turns gray
You're not too old when your teeth decay.
But you'll know you're awaiting that final sleep,
When your mind makes promises your body can't
keep.

You are never too old to set another goal or to dream a new dream.

—Les Brown

May you live to be a hundred—and may the last voice you hear be mine.

May your shadow never grow less.

Remember—you're only young once—but you can stay immature forever.

✳ ✳ ✳

Age appears to be the best in four things—old wood best to burn, old wine to drink, old friends to trust, and old authors to read.

—Francis Bacon

King's Peg

2 parts cognac (2 oz.)
Chilled champagne

Divide cognac between two champagne flutes. Fill with chilled champagne and stir gently.

Serves 2

Births

There is nothing as fragile and beautiful as a newborn child. Whether it's your first child or your hundredth grandchild—the thrill is never gone. Births are a classic occasion to raise a glass and say something poignant. Even if you feel the world is too crazy a place for children, just think, at least you'll have someone new to commiserate with. And now that Mom can drink again you'll want to have a little something more to say than, "Thanks for the baby, Mabel."

 See also: Family, page 77,
Fathers & Fatherhood, page 81,
Mothers & Motherhood, page 151.

* * *

Golden slumbers kiss your eyes,
Smiles awake you when you rise
Sleep, pretty wantons, do not cry,
And I will sing a lullaby.

—Thomas Decker

Every baby born into the world is a finer one than
the last.

—Charles Dickens

Begin at once to live, and count each separate
day as a separate life.

—Seneca

Forasmuch as it hath pleased Almighty God
of his goodness to give you safe deliverance
and hath preserved you in the great danger
of Child-birth: you shall therefore give hearty
thanks unto God.

(Book of Common Prayer)

A new life begun,
Like father, like son.

One generation passeth away, and another
generation cometh: but the earth abideth for ever.
The sun also ariseth, and the sun goeth down,
and hasteth to the place where he arose.

(Ecclesiastes 1:4–5)

To the new baby—who will show his/her parents
the perfect example of minority rule!

Every child comes with the message that God is
not yet discouraged of man.

—Rabindranath Tagore

You may give them your love but not your
    thoughts.
For they have their own thoughts.
You may house their bodies but not their souls,
For their souls dwell in the house of tomorrow,
    which
You cannot visit, not even in your dreams.

—Kahlil Gibran

Don't throw the baby out with the bathwater.

(proverb)

The proper time to influence the character of a
child is about a hundred years before he is born.

—William Ralph Inge

Here's to baby, man to be—
May he be as fine as thee.

When we are born, we cry that we are come
To this great stage of fools.

—William Shakespeare

A baby will make love stronger,
Days shorter, Nights longer,
Your bankroll smaller, home happier,
Your clothes shabbier, the past forgotten,
and the future worth living for.

Where'er you walk, cool gales shall fan the glade,
Trees, where you sit, shall crowd into a shade:
Where'er you tread, the blushing flow'rs shall rise,
And all things flourish where you turn your eyes.

—Alexander Pope

Like one, like the other,
Like daughter, like mother.

But what am I?
An infant crying in the night:
And infant crying for the light:
And with no language but a cry.

—Alfred, Lord Tennyson

Father of fathers, make me one,
A fit example for a son.
A lovely being scarcely formed or molded,
A rose with all it's sweetest leaves yet folded

—George Gordon, Lord Byron

Here's to baby, woman to be—
May she be as sweet as thee.

Train up a child in the way he should go: and
when he is old, he will not depart from it.

(Proverbs 22:6)

May your children's parents be rich!

"The stork has brought a little peach"
The nurse said with an air.
"I'm mighty glad," the father said,
"He didn't bring a pear."

A generation of children on the children of your
children.

(Irish blessing)

Children are poor men's riches.

(English proverb)

Grandchildren are gifts from above.
It's God's way of compensating the aging process.

(Irish saying)

May the child grow to twice as tall as you and
half as wise.

(Irish saying)

Blessings & Proverbs

It's easy to add an air of beauty and poignancy to a shared drink with these toasts. While many are taken from scripture, feel free to change the language to fit your belief system. Even if you're an atheist, the sentiments can be adapted and still be considered beautiful and moving.

Teach us Delight in simple things,
And Mirth that has no bitter springs.

—Rudyard Kipling

Almighty God, give us the grace that we may cast away the works of darkness, and put upon us the armor of light, now in the time of this mortal life.

(Book of Common Prayer)

The earth never tires;

The earth is rude, silent, incomprehensible at
 first—Nature is rude and incomprehensible
 at first;

Be not discouraged—keep on—there are divine
 things, well envelop'd;

I swear to you there are divine things more
 beautiful than words can tell.

—Walt Whitman

Establish in some better way
My life, thou Godhead! that I may
Know it as virtue ranks
To scorn Thy gifts, or give Thee thanks.

—John Eglinton

With God I have no fears.
And round me roll His seas.

—Wilfred Roland Childe

Lord have mercy upon us

(Book of Common Prayer)

[We pray to you], O God,
For strength, determination, and willpower,
to do instead of just to pray,
To become instead of merely to wish

—Harold S. Kushner

Let the thankful heart sweep through the day
and, as the magnet finds the iron, so it will find,
in every hour, some heavenly blessings!

—Henry Ward Beecher

The Lord bless thee, and keep thee:
The Lord make his face shine upon thee, and be
gracious unto thee:
The Lord lift up his countenance upon thee, and
give thee peace.
(Numbers 6:24–26)

I have three treasures. Guard and keep them:
The first is deep love,
The second is frugality,
And the third is not to dare to be ahead of the
world.
Because of deep love, one is courageous.
Because of frugality, one is generous.
Because of not daring to be ahead of the world,
One becomes the leader of the world.

—Lao-tzu

Grant that this day we fall into no sin, neither run
into any kind of danger.

(Book of Common Prayer)

When I first open my eyes upon the morning
meadows and look out upon the beautiful world, I
thank God I am alive.
—Ralph Waldo Emerson

As it was in the beginning, is now, and ever shall be: world without end.

(Book of Common Prayer)

Just to be is a blessing. Just to live is holy.

—Abraham Heschel

There is no evil like hatred,
And no fortitude like patience.

(Buddhist proverb)

O let the Earth bless the Lord: yea, let it praise him. And magnify him forever.

(Book of Common Prayer)

Drink deeply. Live in serenity and joy.

—Buddha

He who knows others is wise;
He who knows himself is enlightened.

—Lao-tzu

* * *

Avoid what is evil; do what is good; purify the mind—this is the teaching of the Awakened One.

—Buddha

As the proverb says, "a good beginning is half the business" and "to have begun well" is praised by all.

—Plato

He that is of merry heart hath a continual feast.

One who is serious all day will never have a good time, while one who is frivolous all day will never establish a household.

—Ptahhotpe

Righteousness exalteth a nation.

Walk too fast and stumble over nothing.

We learn by teaching.

(Latin proverb)

* * *

It is better to give one shilling than to lend twenty.

* * *

Lucky men need no counsel.

* * *

Give neither counsel nor salt till you are asked for it.

He that lives in hope dances without music.

Follow your desire as long as you live and do not
perform more than is ordered; do not lessen the
time of following desire, for the wasting of time is
an abomination to the spirit. . . . When riches are
gained, follow desire, for riches will not profit if
one is sluggish.

—Ptahhotpe

Fearlessness, singleness of soul, the will
Always to strive for wisdom; opened hand
And governed appetites; and piety
And love of lonely study; humbleness,
Uprightness, heed to injure nought which lives,
Truthfulness, slowness unto wrath, a mind
That lightly letteth go what others prize;
And equanimity, and charity
Which spieth no man's faults; and tenderness
Towards all that suffer; a contented heart,
Fluttered by no desires; a bearing mild,
Modest, and grave, with manhood nobly mixed
With patience, fortitude, and purity;
An unrevengeful spirit, never given
To rate itself too high;—such be the signs,
. . . of him whose feet are set
On that fair path which leads to heavenly birth!

(Bhagavad Gita)

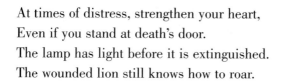

At times of distress, strengthen your heart,
Even if you stand at death's door.
The lamp has light before it is extinguished.
The wounded lion still knows how to roar.

—Samuel ha-Nagid

The fool laughs at generosity.
The miser cannot enter heaven.
But the master finds joy in giving
And happiness in his reward.

(*Dhammapada*)

Remain close to the Great Spirit.
Show great respect to your fellow beings.
Give assistance and kindness whenever needed.
Be truthful and honest at all times.
Do what you know to be right.
Look after the well-being of mind and body.
Treat the Earth and all that dwells thereon with
    respect.
Take full responsibility for your thoughts, words
    and deeds.
Dedicate a share of your efforts to the greater
    good.
Work together for the benefit of mankind.

(Native American Ten Commandments)

In doubt if an action is just; abstain.

—Zoroaster

Whoso has done an atom's weight of good shall
see it; and whoso has done an atom's weight of
evil shall see it.

(Koran)

He who knows does not speak.
He who speaks does not know.

—Lao-tzu

God moves in a mysterious way,
His wonders to perform;
He plants his footsteps in the sea,
And rides upon the storm.

—William Cowper

Whosoever surrenders his face to God and
performs good deeds, he verily has grasped the
surest handle, and unto God is the sequel
of all things.

(Koran)

Manifest plainness,
Embrace simplicity,
Reduce selfishness,
Have few desires.

—Lao-tzu

An honest God is the noblest work of man.

—Robert Green Ingersoll

Teach us, good Lord, to serve Thee
    as Thou deservest:
To give and not to count the cost;
To fight and not to heed the wounds;
To toil and not to seek for rest;
To labor and not to ask for any reward
Save that of knowing that we do Thy will.

            —Saint Ignatius of Loyola

The sage does not accumulate for himself.
The more he uses for others, the more he has
    himself.
The more he gives away, the more he possesses of
    his own.
                    —Lao-tzu

One may know the world without going out of
    doors.
One may see the Way of Heaven without looking
    through the windows.
The further one goes, the less one knows.
Therefore the sage knows without going about,
Understands without seeing,
And accomplishes without any action.

                    —Lao-tzu

Keep a green tree in your heart and perhaps the
singing bird will come.
                (Chinese proverb)

BonVoyage

While I don't suggest having too many
toasts before you go on a long drive,
toasting to a journey, no matter how
short it may be, is a great way to send off
a friend. Whether wishing safe passage and
good times to someone going on vacation
or just walking home from the bar, you'd
be wise to commit some of the following
lines to memory. You'll sound so worldly.

*See also: Blessings & Proverbs, page 35,
International Toasts, page 135, and
New Beginnings, page 155.*

* * *

I have a long journey to take and must bid the
company farewell.
—Sir Walter Raleigh

* * *

When you depart from me, sorrow abides, and
happiness takes his leave.
—William Shakespeare

If I should meet thee
After long years,
How should I greet thee?
With silence and tears.

—George Gordon, Lord Byron

As cold waters to a thirsty soul, so is good news
from a far country.

(Proverbs 25:25)

It's tough to say good-bye to such a good friend,
But I'm sure that we'll meet again.
It always seems to be our luck,
'Cause like a bad penny, you always turn up!

Your absence has gone through me
Like thread through a needle.

—William Stanley Merwin

If we do meet again, why, we shall smile;
If not, why then this parting was well made.

—William Shakespeare

Absence is to love what wind is to fire; it extin-
guishes the small, it inflames the great.

—Roger de Bussy-Rabutin

It is seldom indeed that one parts on good terms,
because if one were on good terms one would not
part.

—Marcel Proust

* * *

At last he rose, and twitch'd his mantle blue,
Tomorrow to fresh woods and pastures new.

—John Milton

* * *

Henceforth I whimper no more,
   postpone no more, need nothing,
Done with indoor complaints, libraries,
   querulous criticisms,
Strong and content I travel the open road.

—Walt Whitman

* * *

I remember the way we parted,
The day and the way we met;
You hoped we were both broken-hearted,
And knew we should both forget.

—Algernon Charles Swinburne

* * *

Must we part?
Well if we must—we must—
And in that case
The less said the better.

—Richard Brinsley Sheridan

Parting is all we know of heaven,
And all we need of hell.

—Emily Dickinson

Good night, good night!
Parting is such sweet sorrow
That I shall say good night till it be morrow.

—William Shakespeare

Nobody likes a long good-bye,
The quicker you leave the faster I'll cry.
But if you speed your departure and leave,
The sooner you'll return and the less I'll grieve.

Every parting gives a foretaste of death; every
coming together again a foretaste of resurrection.

—Arthur Schopenhauer

Come,
Let's have one other gaudy night. Call to me
All my sad captains. Fill our bowls once more.
Let's mock the midnight bell.

—William Shakespeare

Absence makes the heart grow fonder.

(proverb)

Come, once more, a bumper!—then drink as you
please,
Tho' who could fill half-way to toasts such as
these?
Here's our next joyous meeting—and, oh, when
we meet,
May our wine be as bright and our union as
sweet.

All farewells should be sudden, when forever.

—George Gordon, Lord Byron

So, till to-morrow eve, my Own, adieu!
Parting's well-paid with soon again to meet,
Soon in your arms to feel so small and sweet,
Sweet to myself that am so sweet to you!

—William Morris

See you later, alligator.
In a while, crocodile.

Brothers & Sisters

We all know you don't have to be related by blood to be someone's brother or sister. Some "siblings" are simply kindred spirits, or people who've known each other forever and endure each other's bizarre behaviors and annoying idiosyncrasies. Siblings love each other no matter what, and what's more worthy of a toast than that?

 See also: Family, page 77, and Friendship, page 85.

The crest and crowning of all good,
Life's final star, is Brotherhood.

—Edwin Markham

A gentleman nurses the roots: when the root has taken, the truth will grow; and what are the roots of love, but the duty of son and of brother?

—Confucius

A brother may not be a friend, but a friend will always be a brother.

—Samuel Richardson

✳ ✳ ✳

All men are my brethren, and all things my companion.

—Chang Tsai

✳ ✳ ✳

A brother offended is harder to be won than a strong city and their contentions are like the bars of a castle.

(Proverbs 18:19)

✳ ✳ ✳

A pat on the back develops character—if given young enough, often enough and low enough.

✳ ✳ ✳

And much more am I sorrier for my good knight's loss than for the loss of my fair queen; for queens I might have enough, but such a fellowship of good knights shall never be together in no company.

—Sir Thomas Malory

✳ ✳ ✳

If thy brother trespass against thee, rebuke him; and if he repent, forgive him. And if he trespass against thee seven times in a day, and seven times in a day turn again to thee, saying, I repent; thou shalt forgive him.

(Luke 17:3–4)

Here's to cheating, stealing, fighting, and drinking:
If you cheat, may you cheat death.
If you steal, may you steal a woman's heart.
If you fight, may you fight for a brother.
And if you drink, may you drink with me.

If thy brother wrongs thee, remember not so
much his wrong-doing, but more than ever that
he is thy brother.
                            —Epictetus

To hunt tigers one must have a brother's help.

                            (Chinese proverb)

A brother noble,
Whose nature is so far from doing harms
That he suspects none.
                            —William Shakespeare

We came into the world like brother and brother;
And now let's go hand in hand, not one before
another.
                            —William Shakespeare

A sister is both your mirror—and your opposite.

                            —Elizabeth Fishel

A ministering angel shall my sister be.

—William Shakespeare

There is no friend like a sister
In calm or stormy weather;
To cheer one on the tedious way,
To fetch one if one goes astray,
To lift one if one totters down,
To strengthen whilst one stands.

—Christina Rossetti

Surely a gentle sister is the second best gift
to a man; and it is first in point of occurrence;
for the wife comes after.

—Herman Melville

For thee, my own sweet sister, in thy heart
I know myself secure, as thou in mine.
We were and are—I am, even as thou art—
Beings who ne'er each other can resign:
It is the same, together or apart,
From life's commencement to its slow decline
We are entwined—let death come slow or fast,
The tie which bound the first endures the last!

—George Gordon, Lord Byron

Coming of Age

Oddly enough, that step toward adulthood known as "coming of age" can take place at almost any age. You can come of age at an officially sanctioned religious event, like a bar or bat mitzvah or communion, or when you have your first legal drink (and grown-up hangover) at the age of twenty-one. Whatever it is, commemorate the occasion with a toast. It adds that special touch and may even be the first time the person has been toasted! Better make it a good one.

See also: Birthdays, page 13, Graduation, page 105, New Beginnings, page 155, and To Life, page 193.

✳ ✳ ✳

Inexperience is what makes a young man do what an older man says is impossible.

—Herbert V. Prochnow

Speak the truth.
Give whatever you can.
Never be angry.
These three steps will lead you
Into the presence of the gods.

—Buddha

From the earliest times the old have rubbed it
into the young that they are wiser than they, and
before the young had discovered what nonsense
this was they were old too, and it profited them to
carry on the imposture.

—W. Somerset Maugham

Live as long as you may, the first twenty years are
the longest half of your life.

—Robert Southey

***

Youth that rides the wildest horse,
Youth that throws the deadliest steer,
Spending strength without remorse,
Grappling with the ghosts of fear,
Knows it only holds to-day
All it freely flings away.

—Vance Palmer

It is good for a man that he bear the yoke in his
youth.

(Lamentations 3:27)

Take your needle, my child, and work at your
pattern; it will come out a rose by and by.
Life is like that; one stitch at a time taken
patiently, and the pattern will come out all right,
like embroidery.

—Oliver Wendell Holmes

Today you have turned twenty-one
I think that's plain to see
But now at least you will not need
That counterfeit I.D.

Today you have turned twenty-one,
You'll watch your dreams unfurl,
I just suggest you watch your drinks,
So that you do not hurl.

When I was as you are now, towering in the
confidence of twenty-one, little did I suspect that
I should be at forty-nine, what I now am.

—Samuel Johnson

A man that is young in years may be old in
hours, if he has lost no time.

—Francis Bacon

Searching is half the fun: life is much more
manageable when thought of as a scavenger hunt
as opposed to a surprise party.

—Jimmy Buffett

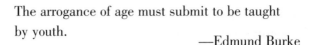

The arrogance of age must submit to be taught by youth.

—Edmund Burke

My advice to you is not to inquire why or whither, but just to enjoy your ice cream while it's on your plate.

—Thornton Wilder

Dare to be wrong, and to dream.

—Friedrich von Schiller

Champagne Cocktail

2 sugar cubes
Several dashes Angostura bitters
Chilled champagne
Lemon twists

Divide the sugar cubes between two chilled champagne flutes. Douse each cube with bitters. Fill each glass with chilled champagne and stir gently. Garnish each with a lemon twist.

Serves 2

Drinking

Alcohol has been humankind's friend and foe since civilization began. No wonder there are such great quotes about it. So when you run out of things to toast to, drink to drinking. Sometimes it's just nice to toast to the thing that got you toasty enough to toast to it. Raise your glass for its contents' sake and say these words that others spake!

 See also: Eating, page 73, International Toasts, page 135, and To Life, page 193.

To my dear friends,
We go together
Like cold pizza and warm beer.

Ale, man, ale's the stuff to drink
For fellows whom it hurts to think.

—A. E. Housman

Oh thrice accursed
Be a champagne thirst,
When the price of beer is all we've got.

* * *

Times are hard,
And wages are small,
So drink more beer,
And screw them all.

* * *

Here's to beer.
Here! Here!

* * *

Come sit we by the fireside,
And roundly drink we here,
Till we see our cheeks are dyed
And noses tanned with beer.

—Robert Herrick

* * *

I'd gladly forsake those chic, imported suds
For a cooler packed full of cold sixteen-ounce Buds.

* * *

In heaven there is no beer . . .
That's why we drink ours here.

* * *

Who'd care to be a bee and sip
Sweet honey from the flower's lip
When he could be a fly and steer
Nose-first into a pint of beer?

Here
With my beer
I sit,
While golden moments flit;
Alas!
They pass
Unheeded by;
And as they fly,
I
Being dry,
Sit, idly sipping here
My beer.

—George Arnold

May the beam in the glass never destroy the ray
in the mind.

Let's drink the liquid of amber so bright;
Let's drink the liquid with foam snowy white;
Let's drink the liquid that brings all good cheer,
Oh, where is the drink like old-fashioned beer?

(Nineteenth-century toast)

None so deaf as those who will not hear.
None so blind as those who will not see.
But I'll wager none so deaf nor blind that he
Sees not nor hears me say, "Come drink this beer."

—W. L. Hassoldt

Be one who drinks the finest of ales.
Every day without fail.
Even when you have drank enough,
Remember that ale is wonderful stuff.

And let the Loving Cup go round,
The cup with blessed memories crowned,
That flows when e'er we meet, my boys.
No draught will hold a drop of sin,
If love is only well stirred in
To keep it sound and sweet, my boys,
To keep it sound and sweet.

—Oliver Wendell Holmes

I am so wrapped, and thoroughly lapped of jolly
good ale and old!

—William Stevenson

At all your feasts, remember too,
When cups are sparkling to the brim
That there is one who drinks to you,
And oh! as warmly drink to him.

* * *

You foam within our glasses, you lusty golden
    brew,
Whoever imbibes takes fire from you.
The young and the old sing your praises,
Here's to beer,
Here's to cheer,
Here's to beer!

—Bedrich Smetana

To beer, like hookers in Vegas—cheap, easy, and
plentiful!

Let gentlemen fine sit down to their wine.
But we'll all of us here stick to our beer.

(Old Somersetshire English song)

Drink down all unkindness.

—William Shakespeare

And if the wine you drink, the lips you press,
Ends in what all begins and ends in—yes,
Think then you are today, what yesterday
You were, to-morrow you shall not be less.

—Omar Khayyám

Champagne costs too much,
Whiskey's too rough,
Vodka puts big mouths in gear.
This little refrain
Should help to explain
Why it's better to order a beer!

To ale and lager, my sweetheart too,
I love all three, but most, the brew.

He that buys land buys many stones.
He that buys flesh buys many bones.
He that buys eggs buys many shells,
But he that buys beer buys nothing else.

To beer: A trusted friend and confidant, perfect
with every meal. What more could you ask for
from a liquid?

Here's to a long life and a merry one.
A quick death and an easy one.
A pretty girl and an honest one.
A cold beer—and another one!

They who drink beer will think beer.

—Washington Irving

Let schoolmasters puzzle their brain
with grammar and nonsense and learning;
Good liquor, I stoutly maintain,
Gives genius better discerning.

—Oliver Goldsmith

Good pies and strong beer.

Wine is a mocker, strong drink is raging.

(Proverbs 10:1)

For every wound, a balm.
For every sorrow, cheer.
For every storm, a calm.
For every thirst, a beer.

When we drink, we get drunk.
When we get drunk, we fall asleep.
When we fall asleep, we commit no sin.
When we commit no sin, we go to heaven.
So, let's all drink, and go to heaven.

Some take their gold
In minted mold,
And some in harps hereafter,
But give me mine
In bubbles fine
And keep the change in laughter.

—Oliver Herford

Cheer up, my mates, the wind does fairly blow;
Clap on more sail, and never spare;
Farewell, all lands, for now we are
In the wide sea of drink, and merrily we go.

—Abraham Cowley

Here's to champagne, the drink divine,
That makes us forget all our troubles;
It's made of a dollar's worth of wine
And three dollars' worth of bubbles.

Wine is as good as life to a man, if it be drunk moderately; what life is then to a man that is without wine? For it was made to make men glad.

(Ecclesiastes 31:27)

Lift 'em high and drain 'em dry
To the guy who says, "My turn to buy!"

Bring in the bottled lightning, a clean tumbler, and a corkscrew.
—Charles Dickens

I have fed purely upon ale; I have eat my ale, drank my ale, and I always sleep upon my ale.

—George Farquhar

Fill with mingled cream and amber,
I will drain that glass again.
Such hilarious visions clamber
Through the chambers of my brain.
Quaintest thoughts, queerest fancies
Come to life and fade away;
What care I how time advances?
I am drinking ale today.
—Edgar Allan Poe

Malt does more than Milton can
To justify God's ways to man.
—A. E. Housman

There are two reasons for drinking; one is, when
you are thirsty, to cure it; the other, when you are
not thirsty, to prevent it . . . Prevention is better
than cure.

—Thomas Love Peacock

Some wine, ho!
And let me the canakin clink, clink;
And let me the canakin clink;
A soldier's a man,
A life's but a span;
Why then, let a soldier drink.

—William Shakespeare

Alcohol is nicisasary f'r man so that now an' thin
he can have a good iv himlilf, ondisturbed be th'
facts.

—Finley Peter Dunne

God made man frail as a bubble;
God made Love, Love made Trouble.
God made the Vine; was it a sin
That man made Wine to drown Trouble in?

The bubbles winked at me and said,
"You'll miss me, brother when you're dead."

—Oliver Herford

Back and side go bare, go bare,
Both hand and foot go cold;
But, belly, God send thee good ale enough
Whether it be new or old.

Then fill the cup, fill high! Fill high!
Nor spare the rosy wine.
If death be in the cup, we'll die—
Such death would be divine.

—Lowell

If God forbade drinking wine, would he have
made wine so good?

—Cardinal Richelieu

Give me wine to wash me clean
From the weather-stains of care.

—Ralph Waldo Emerson

Drink today and drown all sorrow;
You shall, perhaps, not drink tomorrow;
Best while you have it, use your breath,
There is no drinking after death.

—Beaumont and Fletcher

Let us have wine and women
mirth and laughter,
Sermons and soda-water the day after.

—George Gordon, Lord Byron

Brandy is lead in the morning, silver at noon, and gold at night.

(German proverb)

A tavern chair is the throne of human felicity.

—Samuel Johnson

Wine brings to light the hidden secrets of the soul, gives being to our hopes, bids the coward flight, drives dull care away, and teaches new means for the accomplishment of our wishes.

—Horace

Fill to him, to the brim!
Round the table let it roll.
The divine says that wine
Cheers the body and the soul.

Over the lips and down the liver,
Come on, whiskey—make me quiver!

—Redd Foxx

Drunkenness is simply voluntary insanity.

—Seneca the Younger

I drink to the health of another,
And the other I drink to is he
In the hope that he drinks to another,
And the other he drinks to is me.

What butter or whisky'll not cure, there's no cure
for it.

(Irish saying)

May our wine brighten the mind and strengthen
the resolution.

We drink one another's health and spoil our own.

—Jerome K. Jerome

If merely "feeling good" could decide,
drunkenness would be the supremely valid
human experience.

—William James

A cask of wine works more miracles than a
church full of saints.

(Italian proverb)

Claret is the liquor for boys; port for men; but he
who aspires to be a hero must drink brandy.

—Samuel Johnson

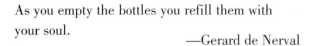

As you empty the bottles you refill them with your soul.

—Gerard de Nerval

Wine improves with age,
I like it the older I get.

Drink to-day, and drown all sorrow;
You shall perhaps not do't to-morrow.

—John Fletcher

When wine enlivens the heart
May friendship surround the table.

May we always be as bubbly as this Champagne!

Eating

Instead of just sitting down for a meal and stuffing your face, try saying some words of commemoration. While eating may seem like a mundane daily event, remember that good food enjoyed with family and friends is always occasion for celebration. Read through these toasts and see how it's done.

 See also: Drinking, page 59.

* * *

Rub-a-dub-dub, thanks for the grub.

* * *

Better is a dry morsel with quiet than a house full of feasting with strife.

(Proverbs 17:1)

* * *

Be known to us in breaking bread,
But do not then depart;
Saviour, abide with us, and spread
Thy table in our heart.

—James Montgomery

Cheers to our host who has provided us with such a delectable meal. Let's break bread together and never break our friendship together.

Oh Roquefort! We accept thee,
With no disgusting note,
As nature's sole apology
For giving us the goat.

—W. E. P. French

* * *

Gourmets dig their graves with their teeth.

(French proverb)

* * *

The sated appetite spurns honey, but to a ravenous appetite even the bitter is sweet.

(Proverbs 27:7)

* * *

The object of dinner is not to eat and drink, but to join in merrymaking and makes lots of noise.

—Lin Yutang

* * *

A full gorged belly never produced a sprightly mind.

—Jeremy Taylor

* * *

He who eats alone chokes alone.

(Arab proverb)

Let's raise a glass to the bountiful feast laid
before us. Surely we do not deserve such
succulent morsels, so let us savor each bite
and never forget those in need.

Up to age forty, eating is beneficial; after forty,
drinking.

(Talmud)

Serenely full, the epicure would say,
Fate cannot harm me, I have dined today.

—Sydney Smith

They eat, they drink, and in communion sweet
Quaff immortality and joy.

—William Shakespeare

Eating while seated makes one large of size;
Eating while standing makes one strong.

(Hindu proverb)

Let the stoics say what they please, we do not eat
food for the good of living, but because the meat
is savory and the appetite is keen.

—Ralph Waldo Emerson

God is great, God is good,
Let us thank Him for this food.

Cauliflower is nothing but cabbage with a college education.

—Mark Twain

A man hath no better thing under the sun than to eat, and to drink, and to be merry.

(Ecclesiastes 3:13)

He was a bold man that first ate an oyster.

—Jonathan Swift

Bless us, oh Lord, and these, thy gifts, which we are about to receive from thy bounty through Christ, our Lord. Amen.

Unquiet meals make ill digestions.

—William Shakespeare

All human history attests
That happiness for man,—the hungry sinner!—
Since Eve ate apples, much depends on dinner.

—George Gordon, Lord Byron

In eating, a third of the stomach should be filled with food, a third with drink, and the rest left empty.

(Talmud)

Family

Families are bizarre—it's that simple. Our relatives know way too much about us and our habits (often more than we know about ourselves). And don't forget that sometimes we have "families" that are made up of our close friends or coworkers —basically people who know how strange we are and still have to deal with us. For that alone, don't they deserve a drink?

See also: Brothers & Sisters, page 51, Fathers & Fatherhood, page 81, Husbands & Wives, page 125, and Mothers & Motherhood, page 151.

* * *

May your home be warmed by the love of your family.

* * *

The family cannot be broken up by a whim.

—Leo Tolstoy

To my family—as they are, so am I.

To our differences,
To our common ground,
To what we search for,
To what we've found,
To what brings us together,
To what sets us apart,
To our special family,
Which shares one heart.

To my family: While our clan may be strange in many ways, it's nice to know I have a loving family when I'm in need. And that may be the strangest thing of all.

Happy families are all alike. . . .

—Leo Tolstoy

Familiar acts are beautiful through love.

—Percy Bysshe Shelley

Your family will always be your home, where you'll find warm words on a cold day.

Here's to us that are here, you that are there, and the rest of us everywhere.

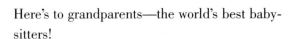

Here's to grandparents—the world's best baby-sitters!

Grandchildren are the crown of the aged,
and the glory of children is their parents.

(Proverbs 17:6)

Let us raise our glasses
And then drink up
To the greatest of folks
Who reared us up!

To Grandma/Grandpa—may our baby's future
be as bright as the gleam in your eye.

* * *

Call her "ant" or call her "aunt"
She says you can when you think you can't!

* * *

To my aunt: My mother's/father's sister, but like a sister to me.

* * *

To my uncle: Thanks for the stuff you let me do,
I hope I grew up just like you.

* * *

Thanks to my uncle, who was always there when I "cried Uncle."

Here's a health to all those we love,

Here's a health to all those that love us,

Here's a health to all those that love them that love us,

Here's a health to all those that love them that love those that love us.

Prince of Wales

2 parts brandy (2 oz.)
2 parts Madeira (2 oz.)
1 part white Curaçao (1 oz.)
6-10 dashes Angostura bitters
Chilled champagne
Orange slices

Combine all ingredients, except champagne and orange slices, with cracked ice in a cocktail shaker. Shake well and strain into two chilled wine glasses. Top both with champagne and stir gently. Garnish each with orange slice.

Serves 2

Fathers & Fatherhood

Aside from the obvious answer to this question, where would we really be without fathers? They inspire us to do great things, push us to fulfill our potential, and embarrass us with their dumb jokes. You've got to give it up for these guys every once in a while, whether you're toasting your own dad or somebody else's.

See also: Brothers & Sisters, page 51, Family, page 77, Husbands & Wives, page 125, and Mothers & Motherhood, page 151.

* * *

Show me the man you honor, and I will show what kind of a man you are, for it shows me what your ideal of manhood is, and what kind of a man you long to be.

—Thomas Carlyle

Father. May the love and respect that we express toward him make up, at least in part, for the worry and care we have visited upon him.

Let us now praise famous men, and our father that begat us.

(Ecclesiastes 44:1)

You gave us life,
You gave us a name,
And for all of our faults,
You're to blame.

What a dreadful thing it must be to have a dull father.

—Mary Mapes Dodge

He that loves not his wife and children, feeds a loneliness at home and breeds a nest of sorrows.

—Jeremy Taylor

Thank you for showing me what it is to be a great man.

When I was a boy of 14 my father was so ignorant I could hardly stand to have the old man around. But when I got to be 21, I was astonished at how much he had learnt in 7 years.

—Mark Twain

To a man who never rested,
But always napped.
Who never was overzealous,
With the strap.
A better father we could never hope,
So here's to your life and your loves old bloke.

None of you can ever be proud enough of being
the child of such a Father who has not his equal
in this world—so great, so good, so faultless.
Try, all of you, to follow in his footsteps and don't
be discouraged, for to be really in everything
like him none of you, I am sure, will ever be.
Try, therefore, to be like him in some points,
and you will have acquired a great deal.

—Queen Victoria

Here's to the man who is wisest and best,
Here's to the man who with judgment is blest.
Here's to the man who's as smart as can be—
I mean the man who's "Dad" to me!

It is not what he has, or even what he does which
expresses the worth of a man, but what he is.

—Henri Frédéric Amiel

He didn't tell me how to live;
He lived, and let me watch him do it.

—Clarence Budington Kelland

Friendship

Friends are truly invaluable. They comfort you when you're feeling low, celebrate with you when you're feeling great, and put up with you when you insist on watching reruns of *Alf* (hey, they might even enjoy it, too). Raise your glass to your buddies, some of the best folks you know!

* * *

The world's best moment is a calm hour passed
In listening to a friend who can talk well.

—Abu 'l-'Ala al-Ma'arri

* * *

Friends are an aid to the young, to guard them from error; to the elderly, to attend to their wants and to supplement their failing power of action; to those in the prime of life, to assist them to noble deeds.

—Aristotle

Some friends play at friendship but a true friend sticks closer than one's nearest kin.

(Proverbs 18:24)

✳ ✳ ✳

Friendship rules the world.

(proverb)

✳ ✳ ✳

All happiness in the world comes from thinking about others, and all suffering in the world comes from preoccupation with yourself.

—Shantiveda

✳ ✳ ✳

At home one relies on parents; away from home one relies on friends.

(Chinese proverb)

✳ ✳ ✳

If all be true that I do think,
There are five reasons we should drink—
Good wine—good friends—or being dry—
Or if we should be, by and by—
Or any other reason why.

✳ ✳ ✳

Here's to you and here's to me,
And if we ever disagree—
To hell with you! Here's to me!

✳ ✳ ✳

Books and friends should be few but good.

(proverb)

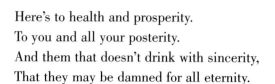

Here's to health and prosperity.
To you and all your posterity.
And them that doesn't drink with sincerity,
That they may be damned for all eternity.

May those who love us love us,
And those who don't love us,
May God turn their hearts,
And if He doesn't turn their hearts,
May He turn their ankles,
So we'll know them by their limping.

Forsake not an old friend; for the new is not com-
parable to him: a new friend is like new wine;
when it is old, thou shalt drink it with pleasure.

(Ecclesiastes 9:10)

If you want an accounting of your worth,
count your friends.
—Merry Brown

I drink to your charm, your beauty and your
brains—which gives you a rough idea of how
hard up I am for a drink.
—Groucho Marx

Here's to our friends—who know us well,
but like us just the same.

Saul and Jonathan were lovely and pleasant in
their lives, and in their death they were not
divided: they were swifter than eagles, they were
stronger than lions.

(2 Samuel 1:23)

* * *

Don't use a hatchet to remove a fly from a friend's
forehead.

(proverb)

* * *

A friend may well be reckoned the masterpiece of
nature.

—Ralph Waldo Emerson

* * *

When you meet someone better than yourself,
turn your thoughts to becoming his equal. When
you meet someone not as good as you are, look
within and examine your own self.

—Confucius

* * *

So long as we are loved by others I should say
that we are almost indispensable; and no man is
useless while he has a friend.

—Robert Louis Stevenson

* * *

Come, landlord, fill the flowing bowl
Until it doth run over;
For tonight we'll merry be—
Tomorrow we'll be sober.

Were it the last drop in the well,
As I gasp'd upon the brink,
Ere my fainting spirit fell,
'Tis to thee that I would drink.

—George Gordon, Lord Byron,
to his friend Tom Moore

The holy passion of friendship is of so sweet and
steady and loyal and enduring a nature that it
will last through a whole lifetime. . . .

—Mark Twain

Now I, friend, drink to you, friend,
As my friend drank to me,
And I, friend, charge you, friend,
As my friend charged me,
That you, friend, drink to your friend,
As my friend drank to me;
And the more we drink together, friend,
The merrier we'll be!

Here's champagne to your real friends and real
pain to your sham friends.

Have no friends not equal to yourself.

—Confucius

A friend is a person with whom I may be sincere.
Before him, I may think aloud.

—Ralph Waldo Emerson

There are good ships,
And there are wood ships,
The ships that sail the sea;
But the best ships
Are friendships,
And may they always be.

To those who like us, and to others like us!

I raise my glass to wish you your heart's desire.

(traditional Russian saying)

The Lord gives us our relatives.
Thank God we can choose our friends.

A friend is a person who dislikes the same people
you do.

Here's to our friends—and the strength to put up
with them.

To our best friends, who know the worst about us
but refuse to believe it.

But the greatest love—the love above all loves,
Even greater than that of a mother,
Is the tender, passionate, undying love,
Of one beer-drunken slob for another.

My friend, if we ever disagree, may you be in the
right.

Here's to the four hinges of Friendship:
Swearing, Lying, Stealing, and Drinking.
When you swear, swear by your country;
When you lie, lie for a pretty woman;
When you steal, steal away from bad company;
And when you drink, drink with me.

Four blessings upon you:
Older whiskey,
Younger women,
Faster horses,
More money.

Choose your friends wisely,
Test your friends well;
True friends like rarest gems,
Prove hard to tell.
Winter him, summer him,
Know your friend well.

We've holidays and holy days, and memory days
   galore;
And when we've toasted every one, I offer just
   one more.
So let us lift our glasses high, and drink a silent
   toast,
The day, deep buried in each heart, that each one
   loves the most.

Come fill the bowl, each jolly soul—
Let Bacchus guide our revels.
Join cup to lip, with Hip! Hip! Hip!
And bury the blue devils.

To our friends: May Fortune be as generous with
them as she has been with us in giving us such
great friends.

Don't walk in front of me—I may not follow.
Don't walk beside me—I may not lead.
Walk beside me. Be my friend.

When wine enlivens the heart, may friendship
surround the table.

The only way to have a friend is to be one.

—Ralph Waldo Emerson

To Friendship—the wine of life. May we always drink of it and to it.

I've drunk your health in company.
I've drunk your health alone—
I've drunk your health so many times
I've nearly wrecked my own.

Long life and happiness—for your long life will be my happiness!

To a true friend—who knows all about me and loves me just the same.

Let us "as adversaries do in law,
Strive mightily, but eat and drink as friends."

—William Shakespeare

My friend, I greet you. And may I never cease to greet you as "my friend."

To friends—as long as we are able
To lift our glasses from the table.

Keep good company and you'll be of them.

To the lamp of true friendship. May it burn brightest in our darkest hours and never flicker in the winds of trial.

Our friends—May you never have to rely on your patience to remain our friends.

Here's a toast from a good friend to my best friend.

Mimosa

Fresh orange juice
Chilled champagne

Fill two champagne glasses half way with orange juice. Add chilled champagne to the top and stir gently.

Serves 2

Funerals

Here are some suggested words to say during a funeral or wake if you are asked or compelled to speak. Sometimes in somber moments like these, it's best to recall the cherished memories of a life rather than remorse at its passing.

See also: Blessings & Proverbs, page 35, New Beginnings, page 155, and To Life, page 193.

* * *

The best portion of a good man's life,
His little, nameless, unremembered acts
Of kindness and of love.

—William Wordsworth

* * *

Lead me from the unreal to the real!
Lead me from darkness to light!
Lead me from death to immortality!

(*Brihadaranyaka Upanishad*)

I have a sin of fear, that when I've spun
My last thread, I shall perish on the shore;
But swear by Thyself that at my death Thy Son
Shall shine as He shines now and heretofore:
And having done that, Thou hast done;
I fear no more.

—John Donne

* * *

Respect death and recall forefathers, the good in
men will again grow sturdy.

—Confucius

* * *

And God shall wipe away all tears from their
eyes; and there shall be no more death, neither
sorrow, nor crying, neither shall there be any
more pain: for the former things are passed away.

(Revelation 21:4)

* * *

Empty your mind of all thoughts.
Let your heart be at peace.
Watch the turmoil of beings,
But contemplate their return.

Each separate being in the universe
Returns to the common source.
Returning to the source is serenity.

(Tao Te Ching)

* * *

There is a land of the living and a land of the
dead and the only bridge is love, the only sur-
vival, the only meaning.

—Thornton Wilder

The death of a dear friend, wife, brother, lover, which seemed nothing but privation, somewhat later assumes the aspect of a guide or genius; for it commonly operates revolutions in our way of life, terminates an epoch of infancy or of youth which was waiting to be closed, breaks up a wonted occupation, or a household, or style of living, and allows for the formation of new ones more friendly to the growth of character.

—Ralph Waldo Emerson

O Lord, support us all the day long, until the shadows lengthen and the evening comes, and the busy world is hushed, and the fever of life is over, and our work is done. Then in Thy mercy grant us a safe lodging, and a holy rest, and peace at last.

—Cardinal John Henry Newman

Time and death shall depart and say in flying
Love has found out a way to live, by dying.

—John Dryden

God does not cause our misfortunes. Some are caused by bad luck, some are caused by bad people, and some are simply an inevitable consequence of our being human and being mortal, living in a world of inflexible natural laws. The painful things that happen to us are not punishments for our misbehavior, nor are they in any way part of some grand design on God's part. Because the tragedy is not God's will, we need

not feel hurt or betrayed by God when tragedy
strikes. We can turn to Him for help in overcom-
ing it, precisely because we can tell ourselves
that God is as outraged by it as we are.

—Harold S. Kushner

Like the dew on the mountain,
Like the foam on the river,
Like the bubble on the fountain,
Thou art gone, and for ever!

The Curfew tolls the knell of parting day,
The lowing herd wind slowly o'er the lea,
The plowman homeward plods his weary way,
And leaves the world to darkness and to me.

—Thomas Gray

Death values a prince no more than a clown; all's
fish that comes to his net; throws at all, and
sweeps stakes; he's no mower that takes a nap at
noon-day, but drives on, fair weather or foul, and
cuts down the green grass as well as the ripe
corn: he's neither squeamish nor queasy stomach'd, for he swallows without chewing, and
crams down all things into his ungracious maw;
and tho' you can see no belly he has, he has a
confounded dropsy, and thirsts after men's lives,
which he guggles down like mother's milk.

—Miguel de Cervantes

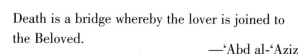

Death is a bridge whereby the lover is joined to
the Beloved.

—'Abd al-'Aziz

We die with the dying:
See, they depart, and we go with them.
We are born with the dead:
See, they return, and bring us with them.

—T. S. Eliot

Ask, and it shall be given to you; seek, and ye
shall find; knock, and it shall be opened unto you.

(Matthew 7:7)

People sleep, and when they die, they wake.

—Muhammad

I died as a mineral and became a plant.
I died as a plant and rose as an animal,
I died as animal and I was a Man.
Why should I fear? When was I less by dying?

—Rumi

* * *

Lord, make me to know mine end, and the
measure of my days, what it is; that I may know
how frail I am.

Difficult times have helped me to understand better than before how infinitely rich and beautiful life is in every way and that so many things that one goes worrying about are of no importance whatsoever.

—Isak Dinesen

There is nothing which at once affects a man so much and so little as his own death.

—Samuel Butler

Friends depart, and memory takes them
To her caverns, pure and deep.

—Thomas Haynes Bayly

Some hang above the tombs,
Some weep in empty rooms,
I, when the Iris blooms,
Remember.

We are not here to curse the darkness, but to light the candle that can guide us through that darkness to a safe and sane future.

—John F. Kennedy

I am going in search of a great perhaps.

—François Rabelais (last words)

Nature made him, and then broke the mold.

—Ludovico Ariosto

* * *

Sleep after toil, port after stormy seas, ease after war, death after life does greatly please.

—Edmund Spenser

* * *

They that sow in tears, shall reap in joy.

(Psalm 126:5)

* * *

The gods conceal from men the happiness of death that they may endure life.

—Lucan

* * *

I told my love, I told my love,
I told her all my heart,
Trembling, cold, in ghastly fears—
Ah, she doth depart.

—William Blake

* * *

It is natural to die as to be born . . .

—Francis Bacon

* * *

All mankinde is of one Author, and is one volume; when one Man dies, one Chapter is not torne out of the book, but translated into a better language.

—John Donne

Verily the life to come shall be better for thee
than this present life: and thy Lord shall give
thee a reward wherewith thou shalt be well
pleased. Did he not find thee an orphan, and hath
he not taken care of thee? And did he not find
thee wandering in error, and hath he not guided
thee into truth?

(Koran)

Men are never really willing to die except for the
sake of freedom: therefore they do not believe in
dying completely.

—Albert Camus

After your death you will be what you were before
your birth.

—Arthur Schopenhauer

I am going a long way
With these thou seest—if indeed I go
(For all my mind is clouded with a doubt)—
To the island-valley of Avilion;
Where falls not hail, or rain, or any snow,
Nor even wind blows loudly; but it lies
Deep-medow'd, happy, fair with orchard lawns
And bowery hollows crown'd with summer sea
Where I will heal me of my grievous wound.

—Alfred, Lord Tennyson

Death to a good man, is but the passing through a dark entry, out of one little dusky room of his father's house, into another that is fair and large, lightsome and glorious, and divinely entertaining.

—Clarke

We understand death for the first time when he puts his hand upon one whom we love.

—Germaine Necker, baronne de Staël-Holstein

Whom the gods love dies young.

—Menander

It is impossible that anything so natural, so necessary, and so universal as death should ever have been designed by Providence as an evil to mankind.

—Jonathan Swift

We picture death as coming to destroy; let us rather picture Christ coming to save. We think of death as ending; let us rather think of life as beginning, and that more abundantly. We think of losing; let us think of gaining. We think of parting; let us think of meeting. We think of going away; let us think of arriving. And as the voice of death whispers "You must go from earth," let us hear the voice of Christ saying, "You are but coming to Me!"

—N. Macleod

Don't cry because it's over. Smile because it
happened.

—Theodor Geisel (Dr. Seuss)

The Lord is my shepherd; I shall not want.
He maketh me to lie down in green pastures:
     He leadeth me beside the still waters.
He restoreth my soul: He leadeth me in the paths
     of righteousness for His name's sake.
Yea, though I walk through the valley of the
     shadow of death,
I will fear no evil: for Thou art with me:
     Thy rod and Thy staff they comfort me. . . .
Surely goodness and mercy shall follow me all
     the days of life:
and I will dwell in the house of the Lord for ever.

(Psalm 23)

Graduation

Black square hats, tassels, scrolled-up pieces of paper, and a perfectly crafted toast—these are the ingredients for a meaningful, memorable graduation day. After all the studying, memorizing, and brownnosing, what better way to celebrate your favorite student's success than with some words of wit or wisdom?

See also: Coming of Age, page 55, New Beginnings, page 155, To Life, page 193.

* * *

Almost everything that is great has been done by youth.

—Benjamin Disraeli

* * *

Know thyself.

(proverb)

Your diamonds are not
in far distant mountains or
in yonder seas;
they are in your own backyard,
if you but dig for them.

—Russell H. Conwell

Confucius said, "A man to whom three years of
study have borne no fruit would be hard to find."
Well, we have a guy here who went to college for
five years and isn't opening up a fruit stand any-
time soon.

Twenty years from now you will be more disappointed by the things you didn't do than by the
ones you did. So throw off the bowlines, sail away
from the safe harbor. Catch the trade winds in
your sails. Explore. Dream.

—Mark Twain

Shoot for the moon. Even if you miss, you will
land among the stars.

—Les Brown

Today is the biggest day of your life;
It's yours and yours alone.
Now go out and tackle the world my friend,
And pay back your student loan.

When you understand one thing through and
through, you understand everything.

When you are hungry, eat your rice; when tired,
close your eyes. Fools may laugh at me, but wise
men will know what I mean.

—Lin-chi

To rank the effort above the prize may be called
love.

—Confucius

The fool that thinks he is a fool is for that very
reason a wise man;
But the fool that thinks he is a wise man is
rightly called a fool.

(*Dhammapada*)

We are what we think.
All that we are arises with our thoughts.
With our thoughts we make the world.

(*Dhammapada*)

* * *

You cannot run with the hare and hunt with the
hounds.

(proverb)

There is only one good, knowledge, and one evil, ignorance.

—Socrates

* * *

The greatest impurity is ignorance.
Free yourself from it.

(*Dhammapada*)

* * *

Education is simply the soul of a society as it passes from one generation to another.

—G. K. Chesterson

* * *

So many worlds, so much to do,
So little done, such things to be.

—Alfred, Lord Tennyson

* * *

The education process has no end beyond itself;
it is its own end.

—John Dewey

* * *

The man of virtue makes the difficulty to be overcome his first business, and success only a subsequent consideration.

—Confucius

* * *

Do not look back in anger, or forward in fear, but around in awareness.

—James Thurber

Upon the education of the people of this country
the fate of this country depends.

—Benjamin Disraeli

I pay the schoolmaster, but 'tis the schoolboys
that educate my son.

—Ralph Waldo Emerson

A gentleman who is not a greedy eater, nor a
lover of ease at home, who is earnest in deed and
careful of speech, who seeks the righteous and
profits by them, may be called fond of learning.

—Confucius

Virtue is more to man than either water or fire. I
have seen men die from treading on water and
fire, but I have never seen a man die from treading the course of virtue.

—Confucius

A wise man is strong; yea, a man of knowledge
increaseth strength.

(Proverbs 24:5)

Oh, the places you'll go!

—Theodor Geisel (Dr. Seuss)

I have never let schooling interfere with my education.

—Mark Twain

Education is an admirable thing, but it is well to remember from to time to time that nothing that is worth knowing can be taught.

—Oscar Wilde

Make one person happy each day and in forty years you will have made 14,600 human beings happy for a little time at least.

—Charley Willey

What we have to learn to do, we learn by doing.

—Aristotle

The ink of the scholar is more sacred than the blood of the martyr.

—Muhammad

* * *

To be able to practice five things everywhere under heaven constitutes perfect virtue . . . [They are] gravity, generosity of soul, sincerity, earnestness, and kindness.

—Confucius

The art of living does not consist in preserving
and clinging to a particular mode of happiness,
but in allowing happiness to change its form
without being disappointed by the change; happiness, like a child, must be allowed to grow up.

—Charles L. Morgan

And still they gazed, and still the wonder grew,
That one small head could carry all he knew.

—Oliver Goldsmith

What sculpture is to a block of marble, education
is to an human soul.

—Joseph Addison

Let your boat of life be light, packed with only
what you need—a homely home and simple
pleasures, one or two friends, worth the name,
someone to love and someone to love you, a cat, a
dog, and a pipe or two, enough to eat and enough
to wear, and a little more than enough to drink;
for thirst is a dangerous thing.

—Jerome K. Jerome

Education makes a people easy to lead, but
difficult to drive; easy to govern but impossible
to enslave.

—Henry Peter, Lord Brougham

The only fence against the world is a thorough knowledge of it.

—John Locke

* * *

One does not "find oneself" by pursuing one's self, but on the contrary by pursuing something else and learning through some discipline or routine (even the routine of making beds) who one is and wants to be.

—May Sarton

* * *

Life is a great big canvas, and you should throw all the paint on it you can.

—Danny Kaye

Kir Royale

4 parts crème de cassis (4 oz.)
Chilled champagne

Stir the cassis with cracked ice in a mixing glass. Strain into two champagne flutes and top with chilled champagne. Stir gently.

Serves 2

Holidays, Seasons & Special Guests

Chestnuts roasting, turkey gobbling, jack-o'-lanterns glowing, beach umbrellas opening . . . whatever the season or holiday, you can always take a moment and make it more meaningful with a toast. Even a brief one-liner can add a special touch to the occasion and will hopefully give your fellow toasters a moment to reflect and appreciate the season—and also what a fabulous toastmaster you are.

See also: Blessings & Proverbs, page 35, Family, page 77, Friendship, page 85, and Patriotism, page 165.

New Year's & Winter Holidays

✴ ✴ ✴

Pour the bubbly, lift the toddy, Happy New Year everybody!

Should auld acquaintance be forgot,
And never brought to min'?
Should auld acquaintance be forgot,
And days o' lang syne?
. . .

For auld lang syne, my dear,
For auld lang syne,
We'll take a cup of kindness yet
For auld lang syne.

—Robert Burns

* * *

In the year ahead may we treat our friends with
kindness and our enemies with generosity.

* * *

May we keep our friends longer than our New
Year's resolutions.

* * *

Welcome be ye that are here,
Welcome all, and make good cheer,
Welcome all, another year.

* * *

Ring out the old, ring in the new,
Ring, happy bells, across the snow:
The year is going, let him go;
Ring out the false, ring in the true.

—Alfred, Lord Tennyson

* * *

Here's to us all! God bless us every one!

—Charles Dickens

Come home with me a little space
And browse about our ancient place,
Lay by your wonted troubles here
And have a turn of Christmas cheer.

—Leslie Pinckney Hill

I heard the bells on Christmas Day
Their old familiar carols play,
And wild and sweet
The words repeat
Of peace on earth good-will to men!

—Henry Wadsworth Longfellow

One word, ere yet the evening ends,
Let's close it with a parting rhyme,
And pledge a hand to all young friends,
As fits the merry Christmas-time.
On life's wide scene you, too, have parts,
That Fate ere long shall bid you play;
Good night! with honest gentle hearts
A kindly greeting go always!

—William Makepeace Thackeray

Now, thrice welcome, Christmas!
Which brings us good cheer,
Mince pies and plum pudding—
Strong ale and strong beer!

Here's to ivy and holly hanging up,
And to something sweet in every cup.

It is very nice to think
The world is full of meat and drink,
With little children saying grace
In every Christian kind of place.

—Robert Louis Stevenson

* * *

Be merry all, be merry all,
With holly dress the festive hall;
Prepare the song, the feast, the ball.
To welcome Merry Christmas.

—Edmund Spenser

* * *

L'Chayim

To Life

(Hebrew saying)

* * *

To unity in the family, community, nation, and race.

(Kwanzaa toast)

* * *

To our people and heritage!

(Kwanzaa toast)

* * *

May we always be one.

(Kwanzaa toast)

St. Patrick's Day

Saint Patrick was a gentleman,
Who, thro' strategy and stealth,
Drove all the snakes from Ireland—
Here's a bumper to his health.
But not too many bumpers,
Lest we lose ourselves, and then
Forget the good Saint Patrick,
And see the snakes again.

Here's to the dear old land
With love and tears and a smile!
Here's to Irish beauty, wit and hearts,
Here's to the luck of the Emerald Isle.

Here's to the land of shamrock so green,
Here's to each lad and his darling colleen,
Here's to the ones we love dearest and most,
And may God bless old Ireland!—that's an
Irishman's toast.

Health and a long life to you.
Land without rent to you.
A child every year to you.
And if you can't go to heaven,
May you at least die in Ireland.

Thanksgiving

* * *

The American Eagle and the Thanksgiving
    Turkey:
May one give us peace in all our states,
And the other a piece for all our plates.

* * *

Here's to the turkey we're about to eat,
and the turkeys we're eating with.

* * *

Here's to a full belly, a heavy purse, and a light
heart.

Valentine's Day

* * *

Now what is love? I pray thee, tell.
It is that fountain and that well.
Where pleasure and repentance dwell.
It is perhaps that saucing bell.
That tolls all in to heaven or hell:
And this is love, as I hear tell.

—Sir Walter Raleigh

* * *

May we kiss those we please and please those we
kiss.

Fair is my Love and cruel as she's fair;
Her brow-shades frown, although her eyes are
    sunny,
Her smiles are lightning, though her pride
    despair,
And her disdains are gall, her favours honey:
A modest maid, deck'd with a blush of honour,
Whose feet do tread green paths of youth and
    love;
The wonder of all eyes that look upon her,
Sacred on earth, design'd a Saint above.

—Samuel Daniel

Was this the face that launch'd a thousand ships
And burnt the topless tower of Ilium?
Sweet Helen, make me immortal with a kiss.

—Christopher Marlowe

Die when you will, you need to wear
At Heaven's court a form more fair
Than beauty here on earth has given: —
Keep but the lovely looks we see,
The voice we hear and you will be
An angel ready made for Heaven.

—Thomas Moore

To a good young girl, but not too good, because
only the good die young.

To old wine and young women.

* * *

Fair and fair, and twice so fair,
As fair as any may be;
Thy love is fair for thee alone,
And for no other lady.

—George Peele

* * *

Whatever you do, stamp out abuses, and love
those who love you.

—Voltaire

* * *

Fair is my love, when her fair golden hairs
With the loose wind ye waving chance to mark;
Fair, when the rose in her red cheeks appears;
Or in her eyes the fire of love does spark.

—Edmund Spenser

Seasons

* * *

Too green the springing April grass,
Too blue the silver speckled sky,
For me to linger here, alas,
While happy winds go laughing by,
Wasting the golden hours indoors,
Washing windows and scrubbing floors.

—Claude McKay

Tired we are of summer,
Tired of gaudy glare,
Showers soft and steaming,
Hot and breathless air.
Tired of listless dreaming,
Through the lazy day:
Jovial wind of winter
Turn us out to play!

—Charles Kingsley

There's joy in the mountains;
There's life in the fountains;
Small clouds are sailing,
Blue sky prevailing;
The rain is over and gone!

—William Wordsworth

Put forth thy leaf, thou lofty plane,
East wind and frost are safely gone;
With zephyr mild and balmy rain
The summer comes serenely on;
Earth, air, and sun and skies combine
To promise all that's kind and fair . . .

—Arthur Hugh Clough

In summer, when the days were long,
We walk'd, two friends, in field and wood;
Our heart was light, our step was strong,
And life lay round us, fair as good,
In summer, when the days were long.

—Wathen Mark Wilks Call

O heart of Spring!
Spirit of light and love and joyous day

—John Shaw Neilson

The closing of an Autumn evening is like the
   running of a hound across the moor.
Night is a good herd: she brings all creatures
   home.

Summer fading, winter comes—
Frosty mornings, tingling thumbs
Window robins, winter rooks,
And the picture story-books.

—Robert Louis Stevenson

Be through my lips to unawaken'd earth
The trumpet of a prophecy! O Wind,
If Winter comes, can Spring be far behind?

—Percy Bysshe Shelley

Special Guests

Be not forgetful to entertain strangers: for thereby
some have entertained angels unawares.

(Hebrews 13:1–2)

＊ ＊ ＊

Guests always bring pleasure: if not the arrival,
the departure.

(proverb)

＊ ＊ ＊

Come in the evening, or come in the morning—
Come when you're looked for, or come without
    warning;
A thousand welcomes you'll find here before you!
And the oftener you come here the more I'll
    adore you!

—Thomas Osborne Davis

＊ ＊ ＊

See, your guests approach;
Address yourself to entertain them sprightly,
And let's be red with mirth.

—William Shakespeare

Husbands & Wives

Some couples are like peanut butter and jelly; others, like oil and water. Either way, it's worth celebrating a duo's similarities and differences. After all, there's a reason a spouse is called a "better half."

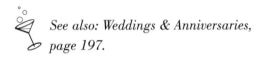

See also: Weddings & Anniversaries, page 197.

* * *

Husbands, love your wives, and be not bitter against them.

(Colossians 3:19)

* * *

Ah, I have loved him too much not to hate him!

—Jean Racine

* * *

All great men are in some degree inspired.

—Cicero

Husbands never become good. They merely become proficient.

—H. L Mencken

He is so good that he is good for nothing.

(Italian proverb)

The majority of husbands remind me of an orang-utan trying to play the violin.

—Honoré de Balzac

What a delight to have a husband at night beside you; were it for nothing than the pleasure of having one to salute you and say, God protect you, when you sneeze.

—Molière

Men are but children, too, though they have gray hairs; they are only of a larger size.

—Seneca

* * *

The real difference between men is energy. A strong will, a settled purpose, an invincible determination, can accomplish almost anything; and in this lies the distinction between great men and little men.

—Thomas Fuller

Marriage is the only adventure open to the coward.

—Voltaire

* * *

Every woman should marry—and no man.

—Benjamin Disraeli

* * *

A man's ledger does not tell what he is, or what he is worth. Count what is in man, not what is on him, if you would know what he is worth— whether rich or poor.

—Henry Ward Beecher

* * *

The gentlemen—divide our time, double our cares, and triple our troubles.

* * *

What a piece of work is man!
How noble in reason! How infinite in faculties!
In form and moving, how express and admirable!
In action, how like an angel! In apprehension, how like a god!

—William Shakespeare

* * *

Here is to man—he is like a kerosene lamp; he is not especially bright; he is often turned down; he generally smokes; and frequently goes out at night.

Breathes there a man with hide so tough
Who says two sexes aren't enough?

—Samuel Hoffenstein

The only time that most women give their orating
husbands undivided attention is when the old
boys mumble in their sleep.

—Walter Mizner

A man who enters his wife's dressing room is
either a philosopher or a fool.

—Honoré de Balzac

A wife as tender, and as true withal,
As the first woman was before her fall;
Made for the man, of whom she is a part,
Made to attract his eyes and keep his heart!

—John Dryden

I would not give my Irish wife
For all the dames of the Saxon land;
I would not give my Irish wife
For the Queen of France's hand;
For she to me is dearer
Than castles strong, or lands, or life:
An outlaw—so I'm near her
To love till death my Irish wife.

—Thomas D'Arcy McGee

Wives are a young men's mistresses, companions for middle age, and old men's nurses.

—Francis Bacon

The wife hath not power over her own body, but the husband: and likewise also the husband hath not power over his own body, but the wife.

(1 Corinthians 7:4)

There is one thing more exasperating than a wife who can cook and won't, and that is the wife who can't cook and will.

—Robert Frost

When a wife loves her husband, he can make her do anything she wants to do.

Ah, my beloved, fill the cup that clears
Today of past regrets and future fears;
Tomorrow!—why, tomorrow I may be
Myself with yesterday's sev'n thousand years!

—Omar Khayyám

There are three faithful friends: an old wife, an old dog, and ready money.

—Benjamin Franklin

Come, messmates, fill the cheerful bowl!
To-night let no one fail,
No matter how the billows roll,
Or roars the ocean gale.
There's toil and danger in our lives,
But let us jovial be,
And drink to sweethearts and to wives
On Saturday night at sea!

＊ ＊ ＊

She wavers, she hesitates; in a word, she is a
woman.

—Jean Racine

＊ ＊ ＊

She deceiving,
I believing;
What need lovers wish for more?

—Sir Charles Sedley

＊ ＊ ＊

Drink to her who long
Hath waked the poet's sigh,—
The girl who gave to song
What gold could never buy!
Oh, woman's heart was made
For minstrel hands alone;
By other fingers played
It yields not half the tone!
Then here's to her who long
Hath waked the poet's sigh,—
The one who gave to song
What gold can never buy!

Women were ever things of many changing
moods.

—Virgil

Brew me a cup for a winter's night.
For the wind howls loud and the furies fight;
Spice it with love and stir it with care,
And I'll toast your bright eyes, my sweetheart fair.

Old as I am, for ladies' love unfit
The power of beauty I remember yet,
Which once inflam'd my soul, and still inspires
my wit.

—John Dryden

Life's a bitch, then you marry one, then you die.

Thoughtless of beauty, she was beauty's self.

—James Thomson

Women are made to be loved, not to be
understood.

—Oscar Wilde

Her beauty makes
This vault a feasting presence full of light.

—William Shakespeare

The wife who drives from the backseat isn't
any worse than the husband who cooks from
the dining-room table.

Drink to me with thine eyes,
And I will pledge with mine;
Or leave a kiss within the cup, And I'll not look
   for wine.
The thirst that from the soul doth rise
Doth ask a drink divine;
But might I of Jove's nectar sip,
I would not change from thine.

—Ben Jonson

Beautiful of form and feature,
Lovely as the day,
Can there be so fair a creature
Formed of common clay.

—Henry Wadsworth Longfellow

Woman: The fairest work of the Great Author;
the edition is large, and no man should be
without a copy.

Women, you can't live with 'em, you can't live
with 'em.

No woman is worth money that will take money.

—Sir John Vanbrugh

Here's to the lasses we've loved, my lad;
Here's to the lips we've pressed;
For kisses and lasses, like liquor in glasses,
The last is always the best.

Drink, drink, drink!
Drink to the girl of your heart;
The wisest, the wittiest, the bravest, the prettiest,
May you never be far apart.

To the Ladies—We admire them for their beauty,
respect them for their intelligence, adore them for
their virtue, and love them because we can't help
it.

Here's to the girl that's strictly in it,
Who doesn't lose her head even for a minute,
Plays well the game and knows the limit,
And still gets all the fun there's in it.

God made the world—and rested,
God made man—and rested,
Then God made woman;
Since then neither God nor man has rested.

International Toasts

This next section will assure that you'll have the necessary toasts for your trip around the world, or your next poker game at the U.N. Here is but a smattering of toasts from around the globe.

AMERICAN:

> Bottoms up!
> Cheers!
> Here's mud in your eye!
> Down the hatch!

ARABIC:
Belsalamati Kah-sahk   Your cup.

BELGIAN:
Op Uw Gezenheid   To your health.

CHINESE:
Kan pi   Empty your cup.

CZECH:
Na zdravi   Health.

DUTCH:
Proost   Cheers!

ESPERANTO:
Ja zia sano   To your health.

FRENCH:
A votre santé   To your health.

GERMAN:
Prosit   Cheers!

GREEK:
Yamas!   To us!
Stin Eyiassou   To your health.

HAWAIIAN:
Havoli maoli oe   To your happiness.

HEBREW:
L'chayim   To life.

IRAQI:
Bisahatik   Long life.

IRISH/SCOTTISH:
Slainte   Health.

ITALIAN:
Alla tua salute   To your health.
Per cent'anni   For a hundred years.
Cin cin   Cheers!

JAPANESE:
Kai pai   Dry cup.

NORWEGIAN/DANISH:
Skaal   Cheers!

POLISH:
Na Zdrowic   Health.

PORTUGUESE:
A sua Saude   To your health.

RUSSIAN:
Za vas   To you.
Za vashe zdorovye   To your health.

SPANISH:
Salud   Health.

SWEDISH:
Skal   Cheers!

Love & Courtship

Love is a subject that has been driving people to drink since Adam and Eve made goo-goo eyes at each other. Whether you're truly head-over-heels about your mate or you're less than inspired and just need a date, it's smart to have a couple of these "lovely" toasts in your back pocket.

See also: Husbands & Wives, page 125, Valentine's Day, page 118, and Weddings & Anniversaries, page 197.

There be none of Beauty's daughters
With a magic like thee;
And like music on the waters
Is thy sweet voice to me:
When, as if its sound were causing
The charmed ocean's pausing,
The waves lie still and gleaming,
And the lull'd winds seem dreaming.

—George Gordon, Lord Byron

My soul is an enchanted boat,
Which, like a sleeping swan, doth float
Upon the silver waves of thy sweet singing.

—Mary Shelley

Beautiful she looks, like a tall garden-lily
Pure from the night, and splendid for the day.

—George Meredith

Not from the whole wide world I chose thee—
Sweetheart, light of the land and the sea!
The wide, wide world could not inclose thee,
For thou art the whole wide world to me

—Richard Watson Gilder

Give all to love;
Obey thy heart;
Friends, kindred, days,
Estate, good-fame,
Plans, credit and the Muse,—
Nothing refuse.

—Ralph Waldo Emerson

She walks in beauty, like the night
Of cloudless climes and starry skies,
And all that's best of dark and bright
Meets in her aspect and her eyes

—George Gordon, Lord Byron

My Love in her attire doth shew her wit,
It doth so well become her:
For every season she hath dressings fit,
For Winter, Spring, and Summer.
No beauty she doth miss
When all her robes are on:
But Beauty's self she is
When all her robes are gone.

Love of a person must extend to the crows on his
roof.

(Chinese proverb)

He who is not impatient is not in love.

—Pietro Aretino

But I, being poor, have only my dreams;
I have spread my dreams under your feet;
Tread softly because you tread on my dreams.

—William Butler Yeats

It is a mistake to speak of a bad choice in love,
since, as soon as a choice exists, it can only be
bad.

—Marcel Proust

Those who are faithless know the pleasures of
love; it is the faithful who know love's tragedies.

—Oscar Wilde

Ill husbandry in love is such
A scandal to love's power,
We ought not to misspend so much
As one poor short-lived hour.

—Charles Cotton

Who ever loved, that loved not at first sight?

—Christopher Marlowe

Love conquers all things.

—Virgil

'Tis better to have loved and lost
Than never to have loved at all.

—Alfred, Lord Tennyson

Love laughs at locksmiths.

(proverb)

* * *

Come, woo me, woo me; for now I am in a holiday
humour and like enough to consent.

—William Shakespeare

* * *

No love like the first love.

(proverb)

Through grief and through danger thy smile hath
    cheer'd my way,
Till hope seem'd to bud from each thorn that
    round me lay;
The darker our fortune, the brighter our pure love
    burn'd,
Till shame into glory, till fear into zeal was turn'd:
Yes, slave as I was, in thy arms my spirit felt free,
And bless'd even the sorrows that made me more
    dear to thee.

—Thomas Moore

My last thought was at least not vain:
I and my mistress, side by side
Shall be together, breathe and ride,
So, one day more am I deified.
Who knows but the world may end to-night?

—Robert Browning

Who can deceive a lover?

—Virgil

Better is a dinner of herbs where love is, than a
stalled ox and hatred therewith.

(Proverbs 15:17)

Love that is not madness is not love.

—Pedro Calderón de la Barca

Love kindled by virtue always kindles another,
provided that its flame appear outwardly.

—Dante Alighieri

Love is imminent in nature, but not incarnate.

—Garnett

Sweetheart, do not love too long:
I loved long and long,
And grew to be out of fashion
Like an old song.

—Willam Butler Yeats

Many waters cannot quench love, neither can the
floods drown it.

(Song of Solomon 8:7)

Cupid: his disgrace is to be called boy; but his
glory is to subdue men.

—William Shakespeare

Lovers' quarrels are the renewal of love.

—Terence

My heart was winter-bound until
I heard you sing;
O voice of Love, hush not, but fill
My life with Spring!

—Frank Dempster Sherman

Suddenly I am still and thou art there,
A viewless visitant and unbesought,
And all my thinking trembles into nought
And all my being opens like a prayer.

— Richard Hovey

There is nothing like desire for preventing the
things we say from having any resemblance to the
things in our minds.

—Marcel Proust

Come to me in my dreams, and then
By day I shall be well again
For then the night will more than pay
The hopeless longing of the day.

—Matthew Arnold

* * *

Passion often turns the cleverest men into idiots
and makes the greatest blockheads clever.

—François, duc de la Rochefoucauld

Love does not dominate; it cultivates.

—Johann Wolfgang von Goethe

Here's to the girl I love,
And here's to the girl that loves me,
And here's to all those who love her whom I love
And all those who love her who love me.

Oh, many and many a young girl for me is pining,
Letting her locks of gold to the cold wind free,
For me, the foremost of our gay young fellows;
But I'd leave a hundred, pure love, for thee!

—Sir Samuel Ferguson

Love, unconquerable,
Waster of rich men, keeper
Of warm lights and all-night vigil
In the soft face of a girl:
Sea-wanderer, forest-visitor!
Even the pure immortals cannot escape you.
And mortal man, in his one day's dusk,
Trembles before your glory.

—Sophocles

A love who is absolutely in love does not know
whether he is more or less in love than others for
anyone who knows this is, just on account, not
absolutely in love.

—Søren Kierkegaard

We are all born of love. It is the principle of existence and its only end.

—Benjamin Disraeli

The visions of the past
Sustain the heart in feeling
Life as she is—our changeful Life,
With friends and kindred dealing.

—William Wordsworth

The lover thinks oftener of reaching his mistress than does the husband of guarding his wife; the prisoner thinks oftener of escaping than does the jailer of shutting the door.

—Stendhal

Let us drink to the thought that wherever a man
    goes
He is sure to find something blissful and dear,
And that when he is far from the lips that he loves,
He can always make love to the lips that are near.

Until yellow Autumn shall usher the Paschal day,
And Patrick's gay festival come in its train
    always—
Although through my coffin the blossoming
    boughs shall grow,
My love on another I'll never in life bestow!

—Edward Walsh

Mysterious love, uncertain treasure,
Hast thou more of pain or pleasure!
Endless torments dwell about thee:
Yet who would live without thee?

—Joseph Addison

Love conquers all things. Let us give in to Love.

—Virgil

Here's to love—sweet misery!

If you win at either love or war, it doesn't mean
the expense has ended.

Men say of women what pleases them; women do
with men what pleases them.
—Sophie de Segur

Here's to the love that lies in a woman's eyes,
And lies, and lies, and lies.
Here's to her eyes, those homes of prayer,
Ah! How they make me think!
I like them sad,
I like them glad.
I love them when they wink.

Why did she love him? Curious fool—Be still—
Is human love the growth of human will?

—George Gordon, Lord Byron

* * *

Perfect love means to love the one through whom
one becomes unhappy.

—Søren Kierkegaard

* * *

She it is who stole my heart,
And left a void and aching smart;
But if she soften not her eye,
I know that life and I must part

—Douglas Hyde

* * *

Love does not consist in gazing at each other but
in looking together in the same direction.

—Antoine de Saint-Exupéry

* * *

Here's to the maid who is thrifty,
And knows it is folly to yearn,
And picks a lover of fifty,
Because he's got money to burn.

* * *

She casts a spell, oh, casts a spell!
Which haunts me more than I can tell.
Dearer, because she makes me ill
Than who would will to make me well.

—Douglas Hyde

To see her was to love her,
Love but her, and love her forever.

—Robert Burns

Drink, drink, drink,
Drink to the girl of your heart;
The wisest, the wittiest, the bravest, the prettiest,
May you never be far apart.

Love lessens a woman's delicacy and increases
man's.
—Jean de la Bruyère

Here's to love—the only fire for which there is no
insurance.

A gentleman in love may behave like a madman
but not like a dunce.

—François, duc de la Rochefoucauld

To our sweethearts and wives—may they never
meet.

***

I know my Love by his way of walking,
And I know my love by his way of talking,
And I know my love dressed in a suit of blue,
And if my Love leaves me, what will I do?

Here's to love and unity; dark corners and opportunity.

Here's to the girl that's good and sweet,
Here's to the girl that's true,
Here's to the girl that rules my heart,
In other words, here's to you.

Drink ye to her that each loves best;
And if you nurse a flame
That's told but to her mutual breast,
We will not ask her name.

—Thomas Campbell

Love is everything it's cracked up to be. That's why people are so cynical about it. It really is worth fighting for, being brave for, risking everything for. And the trouble is, if you don't risk everything, you risk even more.

—Erica Jong

* * *

For where your treasure is, there your heart will be also.

(Matthew 6:21)

Mothers & Motherhood

Without mothers, this world would be a lonely place. You don't have to act like a mama's boy or girl to show your mom you care. All you have to do is have a few kind words for the old lady. Mom always said, "If you don't have anything nice to say, don't say anything at all"—so raise a glass and let your mom know how much you love her.

 See also: Births, page 29, and Family, page 77.

A mother understands what a child does not say.

(Jewish proverb)

Mothers hold their children's hands for just a few short years—but they hold their hearts forever.

When a woman is twenty, a child deforms her;
when she is thirty, he preserves her; and when
forty, he makes her young again.

—Léon Blum

Every one can keep House better than her
Mother, till she trieth.

—Thomas Fuller

There was never a great man who had not a great
mother.

—Olive Schreiner

A man loves his sweetheart the most, his wife the
best, but his mother the longest.

(Irish proverb)

The greatest love is a mother's;
Then comes a dog's,
Then comes a sweetheart's.

(Polish proverb)

Who fed me from her gentle breast,
And hushed me in her arms to rest,
And on my cheek sweet kisses prest?
My mother.

—Ann Taylor

For the hand that rocks the cradle
Is the hand that rules the world.

—William Ross Wallace

✳ ✳ ✳

But the mother's yearning, that completest type of
the life in another life which is the essence of
real human love, feels the presence of the cherished child even in the debased, degraded man.

—George Eliot

✳ ✳ ✳

I want a girl just like the girl that married my
dear old dad.
—William Dillon

✳ ✳ ✳

Whatever else is unsure in this stinking dunghill
of a world a mother's love is not.

—James Joyce

✳ ✳ ✳

A mother is a mother still,
The holiest thing alive.

—Samuel Taylor Coleridge

✳ ✳ ✳

God could not be everywhere and therefore he
made mothers.
(Jewish proverb)

✳ ✳ ✳

To our father's sweetheart—our mother.

New Beginnings

New challenges can be exciting, but sometimes it's a little scary to start from scratch. Show your friend or colleague that you care by creating a thoughtful toast to his or her new path through life.

 See also: Achievement, page 3, Blessings & Proverbs, page 35, Bon Voyage, page 45, Graduation, page 105, New Home, page 161, Promotions, page 181, Retirement, page 187, and To Life, page 193.

＊ ＊ ＊

Life's picture is constantly undergoing change.
The spirit beholds a new world at every moment.

—Rumi

＊ ＊ ＊

The first step is the hardest.

(proverb)

If a man does not make new acquaintances as he advances through life, he will soon find himself left alone. A man should keep his friendships in constant repair.

—Samuel Johnson

God changes not what is in a people, until they change what is in themselves.

(Koran)

I have no spur
To prick the sides of my intent, but only
Vaulting ambition; which o'erleaps itself,
And falls on the other.

—William Shakespeare

Be nice to them on the way up. You may meet them again on the way down.

(Irish saying)

Justice turns the scale, bringing to some learning through suffering.

—Aeschylus

The truth is that the beginning of anything and its end are alike touching.

—Yoshida Kenko

Great oaks from little acorns.

(proverb)

Forsake not a friend of many years for the
acquaintance of a day.

(Irish saying)

If thou art faint in the day of adversity, thy
strength is small.

(Proverbs)

Whoever knows thyself, knows God.

—Muhammad

The spirit of self-help is the root of all genuine
growth in the individual.

—Samuel Smiles

Take account of the difficult while it is still easy,
And deal with the large while it is still tiny.
The most difficult things in the world originate
    with the easy,
And the largest issues originate with the tiny.

Even if my strength should fail, my daring will
win me praise: in mighty enterprises even the
will to succeed is enough.

—Propertius

Love, and do what you like.

—Saint Augustine

If you wish to learn the highest ideals, begin first
with the alphabet.

(Japanese proverb)

Great is the height that I must scale, but the
prospect of glory gives me strength.

—Propertius

Maybe one day we shall be glad to remember
even these hardships.

—Virgil

When you are deluded and full of doubt, even a
thousand books of scripture are not enough.
When you have realized understanding, even one
word is too much.

—Fen-Yang

Give me a firm spot on which to stand, and I
shall move the earth.

—Archimedes

To love oneself is the beginning of a lifelong
romance.

—Oscar Wilde

God helps those that help themselves.

(proverb)

Whenever they rebuild an old building, they
must first of all destroy the old one.
All things at first appear difficult.

(Chinese proverb)

Champagne Punch

16 parts cognac (1 cup or 8 oz.)
16 parts cherry liqueur (1 cup or 8 oz.)
16 parts triple sec (1 cup or 8 oz.)
8 parts sugar syrup (1/2 cup or 4 oz.)
8 parts fresh lemon juice (1/2 cup or 4 oz.)
Champagne or sparkling wine (2 bottles)

Pre-chill ingredients. Pour all ingredients
except champagne into a large punch bowl
with a block of ice and stir well. Just before
serving, add champagne and stir gently.

Serves 15-20

New Home

Moving into a new home can leave a person overwhelmed. Between packing up one place and moving into another, it's easy to misplace your favorite lamp and your sanity. If you're lucky, you'll be toasting to your own new digs; and if you're really lucky, you'll be raising a glass to the pal who's found a place—other than your couch—to crash.

See also: Blessings & Proverbs, page 35, and New Beginnings, page 155.

Home is a name, a word, it is a strong one; stronger than magician ever spoke, or spirit ever answered to, in the strongest conjuration.

—Charles Dickens

Peace be within thy walls, and prosperity within thy palaces.

(Psalms)

No money is better spent than what is laid out for domestic satisfaction.

—Samuel Johnson

Peace be to this house, and to all that dwell in it.

(Book of Common Prayer)

Home is a place not only of strong affections, but of entire unreserve; it is life's undress rehearsal, its backroom, its dressing room, from which we go forth to more careful and guarded intercourse, leaving behind us much debris of cast-off and everyday clothing.

—Harriet Beecher Stowe

I had three chairs in my house; one for solitude, two for friendship, three for society.

—Henry David Thoreau

The ornament of a house is the friends who frequent it.

—Ralph Waldo Emerson

Many a man who thinks to found a home discovers that he has merely opened a tavern for friends.

—Norman Douglas

Home—that blessed word, which opens to the human heart the most perfect glimpse of Heaven, and helps to carry it thither, as on an angel's wings.

—Lydia M. Child

"Home" is any four walls that enclose the right person.

—Helen Rowland

May blessing be upon your house,
Your roof and hearth and walls;
May there be lights to welcome you
When evening's shadow falls—
The love that like a guiding star
Still signals when you roam;
A book, a friend—these be the things
That make a house a home.

—Myrtle Reed

May the roof above you never fall in
And may the friends below it never fall out.

(traditional Irish)

Patriotism

It doesn't need to be Olympics season to toast to your country. No matter where you're from, your homeland is a special place. So wave that flag and celebrate your heritage with your national drink!

 See also: International Toasts, page 135.

The brave old land of deed and song,
We ne'er will do her memories wrong!
For freedom here we'll firmly stand,
As stood our sires for Fatherland!

—Sir Henry Parkes

Our hearts where they rocked our cradle,
Our love where we spent our toil.
And our faith, and our hope and our honor,
We pledge to our native soil.

—Rudyard Kipling

Better than a thousand hollow words
Is one word that brings peace.

(Dhammapada)

Righteousness exalteth a nation.

(Proverbs)

A great nation is like a great man,
When he makes a mistake, he realizes it.
Having realized it, he admits it.
Having admitted it, he corrects it.
He considers those who point out his faults
As his most benevolent teachers.
He thinks of his enemy
As the shadow that he himself casts.

(Tao Te Ching)

Was ever a nation made happy shedding blood
and oppressing? Nay, it is the conquered alone to
whom ills come not, while the mirth of the evil-
doer is changed into wailing.

—Alessandro Manzoni

God has left nations unto the liberty of setting up
such governments as best please themselves.

—Algernon Sidney

Where liberty dwells, there is my country.

—John Milton

166 Cheers!

When Britain first at Heaven's command
Arose from out the azure main,
This was the charter of her land,
And guardian angels sung the strain:
Rule, Britannia! Britannia rules the waves!
Britons never shall be slaves.

—James Thomson

* * *

There are very few so foolish that they had not
rather govern themselves than be governed by
others.

—Thomas Hobbes

* * *

The Lord your God is he that goeth with you, to
fight for you against your enemies, to save you.

(Deuteronomy 20:4)

* * *

My country, 'tis of thee,
Sweet land of liberty,
Of thee I sing;
Land where my fathers died,
Land of the pilgrims' pride,
From every mountain side
Let freedom ring.

—Samuel Francis Smith

* * *

The brave old land of deed and song,
Of gentle hearts and spirits strong,
Of queenly maids and heroes grand,
Of equal laws,—our Fatherland!

—Sir Henry Parkes

Oh, golden-lilied Queen—immortal France!
Thou heritress of storied name and deed,
As thou hast pluck'd, so oft, from cumb'ring weed
The fragrant flow'rs of Freedom and Romance,
So shalt thou seize to-day the fateful chance
That comes to thee in this thy hour of need,
When once again thy sacred frontiers bleed
Beneath the thrust of the Invader's lance.

—Elliott Napier

Our country, right or wrong! When right, to be
kept right; when wrong, to put right!

—Carl Schurz

To freedom from mobs as well as kings.

Dulce et decorum est pro patria mori.
It is sweet and honorable to die for one's country.

—Horace

My country, great and free,
Heart of the world, I drink to thee.

May we love peace enough not to fight for it.

Give me liberty or give me death!

—Patrick Henry

Here's to the Army and Navy,
And to the battles they have won.
Here's to our nation's colors—
May they never run.

* * *

It was wonderful to find America, but it would
have been more wonderful to miss it.

—Mark Twain

* * *

May every patriot love his country, whether he
was born in it or not.

* * *

To America—half brother of all the world!

* * *

May our great men be good and our good men be
great.

* * *

May our leaders be wise and our commerce
increase,
And may we experience the blessings of peace.

Pets

Just because Saint Bernards are the only pets that come readily equipped with toasting materials doesn't mean you can't fill up Fido's dish and share in a drink to your friendship. After all, it is special (let's just hope not too special).

 See also: Friendship, page 85.

The beauty of creatures is nothing other than an image of the divine beauty in which things participate.
                    —Saint Thomas Aquinas

Animals are nothing but the forms of our virtues and vices, wandering before our eyes, the visible phantom of our souls.
                    —Victor Hugo

To his dog, every man is Napoleon; hence the
constant popularity of dogs.

—Aldous Huxley

Love me, love my dog.

(proverb)

If you pick up a starving dog and make him pros-
perous, he will not bite you. This is the principal
difference between a dog and a man.

—Mark Twain

The great pleasure of a dog is that you may make
a fool of yourself with him and not only will he
not scold you, he will make a fool of himself too.

—Samuel Butler

How doth the little crocodile
Improve his shining tail.
And pour the waters of the Nile
On every golden scale!

—Lewis Carroll

I loathe people who keep dogs. They are
cowards who haven't got the guts to bite people
themselves.

—Sir Geoffrey Streatfield

Animals are such agreeable friends—they ask no
questions, they pass no criticisms.

—George Eliot

If a fish is the movement of water embodied,
given shape, then cat is a diagram and pattern
of subtle air.

—Doris Lessing

When I play with my cat, who knows whether she
isn't amusing herself with me more than I am
with her?

—Michel Eyquem de Montaigne

The bliss of animals lies in this, that, on their
lower level, they shadow the bliss of those—few
at any moment on the earth—who do not "look
before and after, and pine for what is not" but
live in the holy carelessness of the eternal now.

—George MacDonald

Professions

It's too bad we have to work for a living, but since we do, might as well raise a glass to one of the many professions. Hopefully none of the sarcastic ones will get you sued or land you in the hospital!

 See also: Promotions, page 181, Retirement, page 187, and Work, page 215.

To our favorite accountant: May you make many brilliant deductions.

To our friend the accountant—the most calculating person we know.

An artist is his own fault.

—John O'Hara

Every artist writes his own autobiography.

—Havelock Ellis

To Monet, Picasso, and our buddy here!

Here's to the banker—the fine fellow who will gladly loan you money when you present sufficient evidence that you don't need it.

To our favorite banker—we're all indebted to you.

Here's to Doctors—raise your drink,
Who cure our chills and ills,
No matter what we really think
About their pills and bills.

A doctor will order you to stop working and rest. Then he hits you with a bill you have to work twenty-four hours a day to pay off.

Honor a physician with the honor due unto him for the uses which ye may have of him: for the Lord hath created him. For of the most High come the healing, and he shall receive honor of the king.

(Ecclesiastes 33:22)

The art of medicine consists in amusing the patient while nature cures the disease.

—Voltaire

Care more for the individual patient than for the special features of the disease.

—Sir William Osler

Here's to Medicine—the only profession that labors incessantly to destroy the reason for its own existence.

No physician, insofar as he is a physician, considers his own good in what he prescribes, but the good of his patient; for the true physician is also a ruler having the human body as a subject, and is not a mere moneymaker.

—Plato

You can always read a doctor's bill and you can never read his prescription.

—Finley Peter Dunne

Whoever rescues a single life earns as much merit as though he had rescued the entire world.

(Talmud)

The desire to take medicine is perhaps the greatest feature which distinguishes man from animals.

—Sir William Osler

A psychiatrist finds you cracked and leaves you broke.

To our friends who manage to care despite managed care.

Doctors are the same as lawyers; the only difference is that lawyers merely rob you, whereas doctors rob you and kill you too.

—Anton Pavlovich Chekhov

Here's to all the lawyers in the room, let me make it a quick toast or else they'll bill me.

If laws could speak for themselves, they would complain about lawyers in the first place.

—Halifax

Recompense injury with justice, and recompense kindness with kindness.

—Confucius

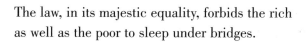

The law, in its majestic equality, forbids the rich as well as the poor to sleep under bridges.

—Anatole France

Laws are like spider's webs: if some poor weak creature comes up against them, it is caught; but a bigger one can break through and get away.

—Solon

Lawyer—One who defends your estate against an enemy, in order that he can appropriate it himself.

Here's to the honest politician—a man who when bought stays bought!

To the politician—a person who divides his time between running for office and running from the law.

To our professor, who talks in his/her students' sleep.

The true aim of everyone who aspires to be a teacher should be, not to impart his own opinions, but to kindle minds.

—F. W. Robertson

The best teacher is the one who suggests rather than dogmatizes, and inspires his listener with the wish to teach himself.

—Edward George Bulwer-Lytton

The teacher is one who makes two ideas grow where only one grew before.

—Elbert Hubbard

Tintoretto

1/2 cup unsweetened pear puree or nectar
4 parts Poire William (4 oz.)
Chilled champagne

Divide pear puree between two chilled wine glasses. Divide the brandy between both glasses and top with champagne. Stir gently.

Serves 2

Promotions

Remember back before you were bitter about your job? Back when you felt like you could make a difference *and* enjoy your life at the same time? Well, when someone starts a new job, let him bask in the new-job glow for a little while. Toast to him while his spirits are up.

See also: Achievement, page 3,
New Beginnings, page 155,
Professions, page 175, Retirement, page 187,
and Work, page 215.

Blessed is he who has found his life's work; let him ask no other blessedness. He has a work; a life purpose; he has found it and will follow it.

—Thomas Carlyle

* * *

In the arena of life the honors and rewards fall to those who show their good qualities in action.

—Aristotle

The world is full of willing people: some willing
to work, the rest willing to let them.

—Robert Frost

Here's to learning the ropes without coming
unraveled.

To a well-deserved award for a job well done.

Nothing is enough for the man for whom enough
is too little.

—Epicurus

Never look for birds of this year in the nests of
the last.

—Miguel de Cervantes

He that leaveth nothing to chance will do few
things ill, but he will do very few things.

—Halifax

Thus times do shift, each thing his turn does hold;
New things succeed, as former things grow old.

—Robert Herrick

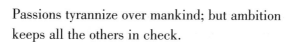

Passions tyrannize over mankind; but ambition keeps all the others in check.

—Jean de la Bruyere

May your luck ever spread, like butter on bread.

* * *

A wise man will make more opportunities than he finds.

—Francis Bacon

* * *

Here's to becoming top banana without losing touch with the bunch.

—Bill Copeland

* * *

Experience is not what happens to a man. It is what a man does with what happens to him.

—Aldous Huxley

* * *

The displacement of a little sand can change occasionally the course of big rivers.

—Manuel Gonzalez Prada

* * *

Not every end is a goal. The end of a melody is not its goal; however, if the melody has not reached its end, it would also not have reached its goal.

—Friedrich Wilhelm Nietzsche

Achievement is the knowledge that you have
studied and worked hard and done the best that
is in you. Success is being praised by others.
That is nice but not as important or satisfying.
Always aim for achievement and forget about
success.

—Helen Hayes

The race by vigor, not by vaunts is won.

—Alexander Pope

The future belongs to those who believe in the
beauty of the dream.

—Eleanor Roosevelt

Prosperity

There's nothing better than a toast to prosperity—especially when your glass is filled with your favorite sale-price domestic beer.

 See also: Achievement, page 3.

Prosperity is the best protector of principle.

—Mark Twain

Here's to our creditors—may they be endowed with the three virtues, faith, hope, and charity.

* * *

Of prosperity mortals can never have enough.

—Aeschylus

* * *

Not everything that can be counted counts, and not everything that counts can be counted.

—Albert Einstein

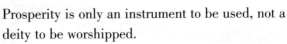

Prosperity is only an instrument to be used, not a deity to be worshipped.

—Calvin Coolidge

May poverty always be a day's march behind us.

Prosperity is the blessing of the Old Testament; adversity is the blessing of the New.

—Francis Bacon

Here's to poverty! It sticks to a man when all his friends forsake him!

Here's to prosperity—Being able to pay a little bit extra for all the things that we don't really need.

Success means we go to sleep at night knowing that our talents and abilities were used in a way that served others.

—Marianne Williamson

Health, contentment, and trust
Are your greatest possessions,
And freedom your greatest joy.

—Buddha

Retirement

Ah, retirement! Congratulate those old codgers with a toast to the good work they've done and the good work that lies ahead of them. They've probably had to make a toast or two in their own careers, so make sure you put this one together with some special care. Good luck.

See also: Achievement, page 3, New Beginnings, page 155, Promotions, page 181, To Life, page 193, and Work, page 215.

May the road rise up to meet you,
May the wind be at your back,
And the sun shine upon your face,
And soft rain fall upon your fields,
And until we meet again
May God hold you in the hollow of His hand.

* * *

Merry met and merry part—
I drink to thee with all my heart.

Good day, good health, good cheer, goodnight.

Amor, salud, dinero, y tiempo para gustare—love,
health, money, and time to enjoy it.

(traditional Spanish)

Happy have we met,
Happy we have been,
Happy may we part,
And happy meet again.

Here's to a man who always kept his feet on the
ground, his shoulder to the wheel and his nose to
the grindstone. How he got any work done in that
position, we'll never know.

Here's to next year's holidays—all 365 of them!

May good fortune precede you, love walk with
you, and good friends follow you.

Here's to the world, the merry old world
To its sky both bright and blue—
Here's to the future, be it what it may
And here's to the best—that's you!

May you always keep a cool head, and a warm heart.

To all the days, now and hereafter,
To happiness, memories and laughter.

When you're sitting at home with nothing to do,
Think of us still at work. We're doing it, too!

To a well-deserved rest for a job well done.

I've drunk to your health in taverns,
I've drunk to your health in my home,
I've drunk to your health so many damn times,
I believe I've ruined my own!

The pain of parting is nothing to the joy of meeting again.

—Charles Dickens

May our lives like the leaves of the maple,
Grow more beautiful as they fade.
May we say our farewells, when it's time to go,
All smiling and unafraid.

—Larry E. Johnson

We work in the trenches
Day after day.
Your friendship makes it worthwhile,
It's certainly not the pay.

A toast to you as you move onward and upward to bigger and better endeavors. We hated to lose you to retirement, but it was the only way we could get rid of you.

I drink as the fates ordain it.
Come fill it and have done with rhymes.
Fill up the lovely glass and drain it
In memory of dear old times.

You're never going to get anywhere if you think you're already there.

Destiny is not a matter of chance, but a matter of choice. It is not a thing to be waited for, it is a thing to be achieved.

—William Jennings Bryan

I didn't realize just how long you had been with the company until we were cleaning out your desk and found a stagecoach ticket.

Many a man has succeeded only because he has failed after repeated efforts. If he had never met defeat, he would never have known great victory.

It is better to wear out than to rust out.

—Bishop Horne

What can you say about a man/woman who is admired, revered, and loved by everyone? I can start by saying he/she's not the man/woman we're honoring tonight.

May you taste the sweetest pleasures that fortune
  ere bestowed,
And may all your friends remember all the favors
  you are owed.

He's afraid nobody will remember him when he's gone. Gee, I can think of several reasons he'll be remembered. He wouldn't like any of them, but I can think of them.

Congratulations on your retirement. It could not have happened to a nicer person. More deserving maybe, but none nicer.

Learn to live well, or fairly make your will.
You've played, and loved, and ate, and drunk
  your fill;
Walk sober off; before a sprightlier age
Comes tittering on, and shoves you from the
  stage;
Leave such to trifle with more grace and ease,
Whom Folly pleases, and whose follies please.

—Alexander Pope

To Life

Dead men make no toasts. While you have it, toast to it.

Too late is tomorrow's life. Live for today.

—Martial

Here's that you may live a thousand years
And I the same but less one day;
For I would not care to live one hour
After you have passed away.

Life admits not of delays; when pleasure can be
had, it is fit to catch it: every hour takes away
part of the things that please us, and perhaps part
of our disposition to be pleased.

—Samuel Johnson

Life without a friend is death without a witness.

(Spanish proverb)

193

Always remember to forget
The things that make you sad.
But never forget to remember
The things that made you glad.
Always remember to forget
The friends that proved untrue.
But never forget to remember
Those that have stuck by you.
Always remember to forget
The troubles that passed away.
But never forget to remember
The blessings that come each day.

Grant me chastity and continence, but not yet.

Here's to life—the first half is ruined by our parents
And the second by our children.

Try to enjoy the great festival of life with other men.

—Epictetus

Life is the art of drawing sufficient conclusions
from insufficient premises.

—Samuel Butler

Life involves passions, faiths, doubts and
courage.

—Josiah Royce

Sound, sound the clarion, fill the fife!
To all the sensual world proclaim,
One crowded hour of glorious life
Is worth an age without a name.

—Sir Walter Scott

Grant me paradise in this world; I'm not sure I'll
reach it in the next.

—Tinteretto

Life is a series of spontaneous changes. Do not
resist them—that only creates sorrow. Let reality
be reality. Let things flow naturally forward in
whatever way they like.

—Lao-tzu

Man's life is but a jest,
A dream, a shadow, bubble, air, a vapor at the
    best.

—George Walter Thornbury

Life is just one damned thing after another.

—Elbert Hubbard

He that no musical instruction is a child in
Music; he that hath no letters is a child in
Learning; he that is untaught is a child in Life.

—Epictetus

To a good man there is no evil, either in life or death. And if God supply not food, has He not, as a wise Commander, sounded the signal for retreat and nothing more? I obey, I follow—speaking good of my Commander, and praising His acts. For at His good pleasure I came; and I depart when it pleases Him; and while I was yet alive that was my work, to sing praises unto God!

—Epictetus

Listen to your life. See it for the fathomless mystery it is. In the boredom and pain of it, no less than in the excitement and gladness: touch, taste, smell your way to the holy and hidden heart of it, because in the last analysis all moments are key moments and life itself is grace.

—Frederick Buechner

Weddings & Anniversaries

Marriage is a subject that seems to beg for a toast. There's no greater testament to love than when two people decide to spend the rest of their lives together for better or worse. Like marriage, the toasts that follow run the gamut of emotions, from inspiring to sentimental to funny to serious. Bless the happy couple—the most successful marriages are still hard work.

See also: Blessings & Proverbs, page 35, Family, page 77, Friendship, page 85, Husbands & Wives, page 125, Love & Courtship, page 137, and New Beginnings, page 155.

May your troubles be less
And your blessings be more.
And nothing but happiness
Come through your door.

Grow old along with me!
The best is yet to be,
The last of life, for which the first was made
Our times are in His hand
Who saith, 'A whole I planned,
Youth shows but half; trust God:
See all nor be afraid!'

—Robert Browning

The Bridegroom's doors are opened wide,
And I am next of kin;
The guests are met, the feast is set:
May'st hear the merry din.

—Samuel Taylor Coleridge

But true love is a durable fire
In the mind ever burning;
Never sick, never old, never dead.
From itself never turn.

—Sir Walter Raleigh

May you never lie, cheat or drink
But if you must lie, lie in each others arms
And if you must cheat, cheat death
But if you must drink, drink with all of us,
because we love you!

When male and female combine, all things
achieve harmony.

—Muhammad

Here's to the prettiest, here's to the wittiest,
Here's to the truest of all who are true,
Here's to the neatest one, here's to the sweetest one,
Here's to them all in one—here's to you.

To keep your marriage brimming,
With love in the loving cup,
Whenever you're wrong, admit it;
Whenever you're right, shut up!

—Ogden Nash

Here's to marriage—The happy estate which
resembles a pair of scissors; so joined that they
cannot be separated; Often moving in opposite
directions, yet always punishing anyone who
comes between them.

Let us drink to the health of the bride,
Let us drink to the health of the groom,
Let us drink to the Parson who tied,
And to every guest in the room.

Marriage is the one subject on which all women
agree and all men disagree.

—Oscar Wilde

To live out of doors with the woman a man loves
is of all lives the most complete and free.

—Robert Louis Stevenson

When a man has married a wife, he finds out
    whether
Her knees and elbow are only glued together

—William Blake

"Marriage": this I call the will that moves two
to create the one which is more than those who
created it.

—Friedrich Wilhelm Nietzsche

Marriage is the highest state of friendship.

—Samuel Robertson

Marriage is popular because it combines the
maximum of temptation with the maximum of
opportunity.

—George Bernard Shaw

I love thee to the level of everyday's
Most quiet need, by sun and candle-light.
I love thee freely, as men strive for Right;
I love thee purely, as they turn from Praise.
I love thee with the passion put to use
In my old griefs, and with my childhood's faith.

—Elizabeth Barrett Browning

May the warmth of our affections survive the frost
of age.

God, the best maker of all marriages,
Combine your hearts in one.

—William Shakespeare

Here is to loving, to romance, to us.
May we travel together through time.
We alone count as none, but together we're one,
For our partnership puts love to rhyme.

(traditional Irish)

May fortune still be kind to you,
And happiness be true to you,
And life be long and good to you,
Is the toast of all your friends to you.

There is nothing nobler or more admirable than
when two people who see eye to eye keep house
as man and wife, confounding their enemies and
delighting their friends.

—Homer

Give me a kisse, and to that kisse a score;
Then to that twenty, adde a hundred more;
A thousand to that hundred; so kisse on,
To make that thousand up a million;
Treble that million, and when that is done,
Let's kisse afresh, as when we first begun.

—Robert Herrick

Love one another but make not a bond of love:
Let it rather be a moving sea between the shores
  of your souls.
Fill each other's cup but drink not from one cup.
Give one another of your bread but eat not from
  the same loaf.
Sing and dance together and be joyous, but let
  each one of you be alone,
Even as the strings of a lute are alone though
  they quiver with the same music.
Give your hearts, but not into each other's keeping.
For only the hand of Life can contain your hearts.
And stand together, yet not too near together:
For the pillars of the temple stand apart,
And the oak tree and the cypress grow not in
  each other's shadow.

—Kahlil Gibran

As sweet and musical
As bright Apollo's lute, strung with his hair;
And when Love speaks, the voice of all the gods
Makes heaven drowsy with the harmony.

—William Shakespeare

Here's to marriage—it's like a cafeteria. You look
the possibilities over carefully, select what you
like the best, and pay later.

May your house always be too small to hold all of
your friends.

The best of happiness, honor, and fortune keep
with you.

— William Shakespeare

Here's to the bride and here's to the groom
And here's to a marriage in full bloom,
Here's to a long and happy life
For a brand new, grand new husband and wife.

It is easy to love the people far away. It is not
always easy to love those close to us. . . . Bring
love into your home for this is where our love for
each other must start.

— Mother Teresa

To the luckiest man on earth—and the woman
who made him that way.

I wish you health, I wish you wealth,
I wish you happiness galore,
I wish you heaven when you die—
What could I wish you more?

Look down, you gods,
And on this happy couple drop a crown.

— William Shakespeare

Love is patient, love is kind. It does not envy, it does not boast, it is not proud. It is not rude, it is not self seeking, it is not easily angered, it keeps no record of wrongs.

(1 Corinthians 13:4)

May you never forget what is worth remembering, or remember what is worth forgetting.

Drink, drink, let the toast start!
May young hearts never part!
Drink, drink, drink,
Let every true lover salute his sweetheart!

—Sigmund Romberg

May your love be as endless as your wedding rings.

May you be poor in misfortune,
Rich in blessings,
Slow to make enemies,
And quick to make friends.

Happiness being a dessert so sweet—
I wish you more than you can ever eat.

May the peace of [God] dwell always in your
hearts and in your home; may you have true
friends to stand by you, both in joy and sorrow.
May you be ready with help and consolation for
all those who come to you in need; and may the
blessings promised to the compassionate descend
in abundance on your house.

—Tertullian

When two people are at one
in their inmost hearts,
they shatter even the strength of iron or bronze.
And when two people understand each other
in their inmost hearts,
their words are sweet and strong,
like the fragrance of orchids.

(I Ching)

May you have warm words on a cold evening,
A full moon on a dark night,
And the road downhill all the way to your door.

This is the miracle that happens every time to
those who really love: the more they give, the
more they possess of that precious, nourishing
love from which flowers and children have their
strength and which could help all human beings
if they would take it without doubting.

—Rainer Maria Rilke

May you have more anniversaries than weddings.

You have become mine forever.
Yes, we have become partners.
I have become yours.
Hereafter, I cannot live without you.
Do not live without me.
Let us share the joys.
We are word and meaning, unite.
You are thought and I am sound.

May the nights be honey-sweet for us.
May the mornings be honey-sweet for us.
May the plants be honey-sweet for us.
May the earth be honey-sweet for us.

May the flower of love never be nipped by the
frost of disappointment,
nor the shadow of grief fall upon you.

(traditional Irish)

May there always be work for your hands to do.
May your purse always hold a coin or two.
May the sun always shine warm on your window-
    pane.
May a rainbow be certain to follow each rain.
May the hand of a friend always be near you.
And may God fill your heart with gladness to
    cheer you.

An anniversary marks time that has passed.
We are celebrating in the present—
with best wishes for the future.
Past, present, future—the best of times!

Now you will feel no rain, for each of you will be
   a shelter to the other.
Now you will feel no cold, for each of you will be
   warmth to the other.
Now there is no loneliness for you; now there is
   no more loneliness.
Now you are two bodies, but there is only one life
   before you.
Go now to your dwelling place, to enter into your
   days together.
And may your days be good and long on the
   earth.

(Apache song)

May your neighbors respect you,
Trouble neglect you,
The angels protect you,
And heaven accept you.
May the Irish hills caress you.
May her lakes and rivers bless you.
May the luck of the Irish enfold you.
May the blessings of Saint Patrick behold you.

(traditional Irish)

May the cooing doves of love never morph into
pecking hens.

To the happy newlyweds—May the newness wear
off but not the happiness.

Here's to the happy couple: May you survive the
wedding and still be in love.

May you be poor in misfortune,
Rich in blessings,
Slow to make enemies,
Quick to make friends.
But rich or poor, quick or slow
May you know nothing but happiness
From this day forward.

May we all be invited to their Golden Wedding
Anniversary.

To the two of you:
Proof that love, like wine, improves with time.

To two people who were made for each other.
Think about it, who else would have them?

To the anniversary couple—living proof of the old
adage that says a good husband makes a good
wife, and a good wife makes a good husband.

Let anniversaries come, and let anniversaries go—
May your happiness go on forever.

Whoso findeth a wife findeth a good thing, and
obtaineth favour of the Lord.

(Proverbs 18:22)

Husbands should love their wives as they do their own bodies. He who loves his wife loves himself.

(Ephesians 5:28)

Wives in their husbands' absences grow subtler,
And daughters sometimes run off with the butler.

—George Gordon, Lord Byron

A virtuous wife is a man's best treasure.

—Muhammad

Here's to you both, a beautiful pair
On the birthday of your love affair.
Here's to the husband and here's to the wife.
May they be lovers the rest of their life.

Immature love says,
   "I love you because I need you."
Mature love says,
   "I need you because I love you."

Love seems the swiftest, but it is the slowest of growths. No man or woman really knows what perfect love is until they have been married a quarter of a century.

—Mark Twain

There's a Chinese proverb that says, "a couple who spend one happy day together are blessed with a hundred days of affection." So by my count, these folks are covered for the rest of their lives.

French "75"

4 parts cognac (4 oz.)
Sugar syrup (2 tbsp.)
2 parts fresh lemon juice (2 oz.)
Chilled champagne
Lemon twists

Combine all ingredients, except champagne and lemon twists, with cracked ice in a cocktail shaker. Shake well and pour into two chilled highball glasses. Fill each glass with chilled champagne and garnish each with lemon twist.

Serves 2

Witty One-Liners

Here are some good one-liners and such that defy categorization. These can serve as retorts in case you find yourself as the subject of a toast or roast, or can just be tossed out there for a laugh or two.

* * *

There is nothing more uncommon than common sense.

* * *

A penny saved is a penny taxed.

* * *

Modern Age—When girls wear less on the street than their grandmothers wore in bed.

Death and taxes may always be with us but at least death can't get any worse.

Life is a battle of wits—good thing this guy's a pacifist.

Socialism becomes popular whenever hard working, thrifty people build something worth owning which other people want.

He that falls in love with himself will have no rivals.

—Benjamin Franklin

Sometimes it sounds like the world is getting worse but I think it's just that the news coverage is getting better.

Hunger is an instinct in man to make sure that he will work.

A diplomat is someone who knows when it isn't safe to laugh.

The lines and wrinkles of a person's face show the twists and turns of his life.

This is a story that only a mother could hate.

Too low they build, who build beneath the stars.

—Edward Young

He's a healthy son of a gun. The kind of a guy who lives till he's a hundred and never uses glasses. Just drinks straight from the bottle.

Acquaintance—A person you know well enough to borrow from but not well enough to lend to.

Luck—A guy bends down to pick up a horse-shoe on the road and a truck comes along and knocks him over a fence into a field of four-leaf clovers.

He who speaks sows; he who listens reaps.

Philanthropist—Someone who returns to people publicly a small percentage of the wealth he has accrued by stealing from them privately.

Work

Sometimes, just getting out of bed in the morning is worth toasting to (if you agree, I suggest toasting with a glass of tomato juice rather than a full Bloody Mary). Even if you're just getting up to cash your unemployment check, that's still work! But hopefully you can raise your glass to a job well done, or a raise, or a promotion, or a new position. Following are some classic turns of phrase to wow your friends and coworkers.

 See also: Promotions, page 181, and Retirement, page 187.

A journey of a thousand miles must begin with a single step.
—Lao-tzu

Never sell the bear's skin until you have killed the bear.
—Jean La Fontaine

In all toil there is profit, but mere talk leads only
to poverty.

(Proverbs 14:23)

Here's the rule for bargains. "Do other men,
for they would do you." That's the true business
precept. All others are counterfeit.

—Charles Dickens

It is not the same to talk of bulls as to be in the
bullring.

(Spanish proverb)

Treat the small as great and the few as many.

(Tao Te Ching)

You pays your money and you takes your choice.

Poverty without complaint is hard, just as wealth
with arrogance is easy.

(Chinese proverb)

Riches are not from abundance of worldly goods,
but from a contented mind.

—Muhammad

Without money, honor is no more than a disease.

—Jean Racine

Money without honor is a disease.

—Honoré de Balzac

Employment is nature's physician, and is essential to human happiness.

—Galen

The almighty dollar, that great object of universal devotion throughout our land.

—Washington Irving

Better to be too skeptical than too trusting.

(Chinese proverb)

Ill fares the land, to hastening ills a prey,
Where wealth accumulates, and men decay.

—Oliver Goldsmith

Idleness begets ennui, ennui the hypochondriac, and that a diseased body. No laborious person was ever yet hysterical.

—Thomas Jefferson

A business that makes nothing but money is a
poor kind of business.

—Henry Ford

If a man look sharply and attentively, he shall
see Fortune: for though she be blind, yet she is
not invisible. The way of fortune is like the
Milken Way in the sky; which is a meeting or
knot of a number of small stars; not seen asunder,
but giving light together.

—Francis Bacon

If your riches are yours, why don't you take them
with you to t'other world?

—Benjamin Franklin

To abandon something halfway is to fail completely.

(Chinese proverb)

Work banishes those three great evils, boredom,
vice and poverty.

—Voltaire

Fortune helps those who dare.

—Virgil

The love of money is the root of all evil.

(1 Timothy 6:10)

Business underlies everything in our national life, including our spiritual life. Witness the fact that in the Lord's Prayer the first petition is for daily bread. No one can worship God or love his neighbor on an empty stomach.

—Woodrow Wilson

It cannot be denied, but outward accidents conduce much to fortune; favor, opportunity, death of others, occasion fitting virtue. But chiefly, the mould of a man's fortune is in his own hands. *Faber quisque fortunæ suæ* [Every one is the architect of his own fortune], saith the poet.

—Francis Bacon

A man's worth is no greater than his ambitions.

—Marcus Aurelius Antoninus

No bird soars too high if he soars with his own wings.

—William Blake

It is not from the benevolence of the butcher, the brewer, or the baker, that we expect our dinner, but from their regard to their own interest.

—Adam Smith

The world is like a great empty dream.
Why should one toil away one's life?

—Li Po

Most people sell their souls, and live with a good
conscience on the proceeds.

—Logan Pearsall Smith

Everyone lives by selling something.

—Robert Louis Stevenson

Study to be quiet, and to do your own business,
and to work with your own hands, as we com-
manded you.

(1 Thessalonians 4:11)

You never find people laboring to convince you
that you may live very happily upon a plentiful
fortune.

—Samuel Johnson

Do something useful and you will have everything you want. Doors are shut for those who are
dull and lazy; life is secure for those who obey
the law of work.

—José Martí

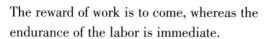

The reward of work is to come, whereas the endurance of the labor is immediate.

—Al-Jahiz

Love your neighbor is not merely sound Christianity; it is good business.

—David Lloyd George

Those who earn an honest living are the beloved of God.

—Muhammad

Every crowd has a silver lining.

—P. T. Barnum

A wise man adapts himself to circumstances, as water shapes itself to the vessel that contains it.

(Chinese proverb)

A man who has a million dollars is as well off as if he were rich.

—John Jacob Astor

If any would not work, neither should he eat.

(2 Thessalonians 3:10)

Make money: make it honestly if possible;
if not, make it by any means.

—Horace

Work is good, provided you do not forget to live.

(Bantu proverb)

Bellini

4 parts peach nectar (4 oz.)
1 part fresh lemon juice (1 oz.)
Chilled champagne

Divide the fruit juices between two chilled
champagne flutes. Stir well. Fill each glass
with champagne. Stir again gently.

Serves 2

Bar Tricks

Guaranteed to Win Friends, Intimidate Enemies, and Earn You Free Drinks!

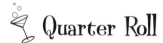 ## Quarter Roll

PROPS: 2 quarters, pencil, paper napkin
GOAL: To make your drinking buddy look like a zebra

Place one of the quarters in your pocket, and the other in your hand under the bar. Rub a pencil or ashes all around the hidden quarter's edge until it is blackened. Use the pencil to draw a large circle on the napkin. Place the marked quarter on the bar, and then wager a drink that your barfly buddy cannot roll a quarter down his face and into the circle on the napkin. Pull out the quarter in your pocket to demonstrate how to do it, then pocket the quarter again. Motion toward the marked quarter on the bar and let your friend try. Each time he rolls the quarter down his face it will leave a black line. Keep this up for as long as you can keep a straight face. (It helps if your drinking buddy is already tanked.)

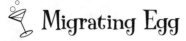

Migrating Egg

PROPS: 1 egg, 2 glasses

GOAL: To move the egg from one glass to the other without touching either

Place the egg in one of the glasses and put it in front of you. Put the empty glass next to it. Announce to your friends that you can move the egg into the other glass without touching the egg or the glasses. Once you have everyone's attention, blow hard into the glass with the egg, and the egg will jump into the other glass! Here's a hint: Practice with a hard-boiled egg at home before you unleash this one on your besotted buddies.

Crazy Suction Cups

PROPS: Small drinking glass, matches, Sambuca

GOAL: To get the glass to stick to your skin

Pour about a tablespoon or so of Sambuca into a small drinking glass. Light it, and then put the palm of your hand over the mouth of the glass to extinguish the flame. As the flame goes out, it will burn up all the oxygen in the glass, creating a vacuum. Once the flame is gone, you can lift the glass with your palm, shake your hand all around, wave to people, scratch your head, etc., without the glass coming off. A word of advice: Before you try this trick, decrease your chance of burning yourself by running your palm under very cold water or rubbing it with an ice cube. And be careful—there's a very fine line between being clever and being stupid.

 # The Race

PROPS: 3 shots of any liquor, 3 pints of beer

GOAL: To fool your friends and bar mates

Bet one of your friends free drinks that you can drink your three pints of beer faster than he can drink his three small shots. The only rule is that neither player can touch the other's glass. Start drinking your beer as your friend takes his first shot. As soon as you finish drinking your first beer, place your empty pint over your friend's third shot. Your friend is not allowed to touch your glass, so take your time and enjoy your free drinks.

 # The Magic Bottle

PROPS: Empty liquor bottle, a flexible straw, matches

GOAL: To make the straw float

Take an empty liquor bottle and run it under very hot water for a minute or so. Bend the straw at the elbow and place it in the bottle so the top is hanging over the lip of the bottle. Light a match and drop it into the bottle. Stand back. Watch the straw float up. **Be careful not to hold your face or any other body part over the bottle while performing this trick.** Here's a hint: Use a liquor bottle that contained high proof alcohol, like 151 rum.

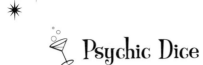 Psychic Dice

PROPS: 3 dice, a glass of water

GOAL: To guess the sum of the numbers on the bottoms of dice without looking at them.

With your eyes closed, ask a bar mate to drop three dice into a glass of water, raise the glass over her head and count the total sum of the numbers on the dice at the bottom. Then, ask her to set the glass back down. Open your eyes. Dip your finger in the water, rub your wet finger on your forehead as if to concentrate, and then reveal the total of the bottoms of the dice. All you have to do is add up the numbers on top of the dice and subtract this total from 21—it works every time!

 Polly's Dollar Trick

PROPS: Empty beer bottle, 1 crisp dollar bill, 4 quarters

GOAL: Using only one finger, remove the dollar without disturbing the quarters.

Take an empty beer bottle and center the dollar bill flat on top of it. Stack the quarters on top of the dollar. Lick your index finger to make it fairly wet. In one swift motion bring your finger down on the dollar, which will stick to your wet finger, and pull it out from between the bottle and the quarters. Be sure to practice this one before going public!

 # Bar Crab

PROPS: Cocktail napkin, whole lemon or lime
GOAL: To make a "crab" crawl across the bar

Open a cocktail napkin. Twist all four ends so it looks like a parachute. This is your crab. Place the crab over a whole lemon, making sure the twisted corners are pointed down like four legs. Push the lemon and watch the "crab" crawl across the bar.

Magic Ash

PROPS: Ashtray with ashes, cigarette, matches
GOAL: To make an ash seemingly jump from your hand to your friend's hand

Without your friend seeing you, dip your index finger into an ashtray so that a bit of ash remains on the tip of your finger. Light a cigarette and ask a friend to face you. Keep eye contact with your friend so that she doesn't see the ash on your finger. Have her extend both hands. Hold both of her hands as if positioning them. Surreptitiously wipe your ashy index finger on your friend's palm. A light touch is sufficient to make the ash stick. Tell her to watch you very closely. Make a loose fist and tap an ash into it with the cigarette. Then ask your friend to do everything she sees you do. Bang your fists together, tap your friend's fists with your fists, hammer the bar with your fists, knock on your head, etc. Then hold your fists out before your friend and ask her to choose which one has the ash in it. When she points to a hand, say nothing and instead point toward whichever of her hands has the ash in it. When your pal opens her fist she'll discover that the ash has magically "jumped" into her hand.

The Amazing Olive

PROPS: 1 olive, 1 brandy snifter

GOAL: To get the olive into the brandy snifter without touching the olive

Place the olive on the bar and put the brandy snifter, open and down, over the olive. Rotate the brandy snifter around the olive, gradually increasing the speed. The olive will roll around the inside of the snifter. Once the olive is spinning around the middle of the snifter, flip the snifter upright. This is a bar classic, yet it never ceases to amaze. Be sure to practice!

Disappearing Water

PROPS: 4 matches, lighter, saucer, water, lemon or lime wedge, highball glass

GOAL: To make the water disappear without touching the saucer

Put a little water in the saucer. Stick four matches (wooden matches work best) in the side of the lemon, sulfur end sticking out. Place the lemon wedge, skin down, on the saucer. Light the matches. Place the highball glass, open side down, over the lemon wedge. The flames will go out and the water will disappear.

Heads or Tails

PROPS: Matchbook, pen

GOAL: To win a free drink

Take one match out of the matchbook. Write "heads" on one side of the match and "tails" on the other. Tell your bar mate that you will toss the match into the air and if it lands on either heads or tails, you'll buy him a drink. If it lands on its side, he'll buy you a drink. Seems he can't lose, right? Wrong! Just before you toss the match, bend it. It will land on its side every time. Cheers!

 Dry Martini

PROPS: Metal cocktail shaker,
absorbent paper towel, strainer
GOAL: To make a truly dry martini

Place a rolled-up paper towel in the bottom of the large cup of your cocktail shaker. Find your favorite martini drinker and offer to make him a very special dry martini. While he watches, pour the vodka or gin, a whisper of vermouth, and some ice into the shaker and shake, shake, shake! Open the mixer, place the strainer over the glass and watch with glee as nothing comes out of the shaker.

Chug-a-Lug

PROPS: Beer in bottles, a flexible straw
GOAL: To chug a full beer faster than
your pal chugs half

Let a friend drink half of his beer, then wager that you can drink your entire bottle before he can finish the rest of his. Once he agrees, take the flexible straw and place it inside your beer, with only the top third of the straw sticking out. Holding the straw to one side, chug your beer. The air escaping through the straw will allow you to drink your beer very quickly.

Pyramid of Quarters

PROPS: 10 quarters

GOAL: To make the pyramid point in the opposite direction by moving only three quarters

Arrange the quarters into a flat pyramid. Place four on the bottom, three above them, two above them, and then one on top. Remove the three quarters at the points of the pyramid. Reassemble them with the point now on the other end. Voila! You have reversed the pyramid!

Egg Float

PROPS: Glass of water, egg, salt shaker

GOAL: To make an egg float

Take a glass of water and carefully drop an egg into it. After the egg sinks to the bottom of the glass, bet your buddy a free drink that you can make the egg float. After she rises to the challenge, shake some salt into the glass, stir, and watch the egg rise to the surface. You've just earned yourself another Mai Tai!

Balancing Beer

PROPS: 2 pint glasses of beer

GOAL: To make your pal look silly

Bet your friend that she can't balance two pints of beer on her hands. Have her place her hands, palms down, on the bar. Place two full pints of beer on her hands. Turns out she can balance the beers! You lose, but your buddy can't move her hands without spilling the drinks!

Two Quarters

PROPS: Two quarters
GOAL: Free drinks

Place two quarters on the bar, heads up. Ask
your barstool neighbor what he sees. He will
most likely answer "two quarters" or "two heads."
Nod your head in agreement. With your palm up,
point to the two quarters and say, "I see two
pennies. Hey, if I'm wrong, will you buy me a
drink?" Pressure your buddy for a reply (most
people will acquiesce). At this point say, "I'm
wrong." Enjoy your free drink. This trick has been
around for decades, yet it always seems to work.

The Vanishing Quarter

PROPS: Shot glass, Rose's lime juice, paper
cocktail napkins, quarter
GOAL: To make a quarter disappear

Behind the scenes, rim a shot glass with Rose's
lime juice. Place the glass, rim down, onto a
paper cocktail napkin. While holding down the
glass firmly atop the napkin, slowly and neatly
rip away the extra napkin around the edge.
This should leave you with a perfect circle of
paper under the open end of the glass. Drape
an unfolded cocktail napkin over the shot glass
to hide it. You are now ready to confound your
drinking mates.

Arrange two napkins in front of your buddies,
placing a quarter on one. Now bring your shot
glass from its hidden position. Put the covered
shot glass, rim down, onto the napkin without the
quarter. Announce to your friends, "I am going
to make this quarter disappear!" Pick up the

covered glass and move it over to the napkin with the quarter on it. Tap the shot glass three times, counting aloud to three. With a flourish, remove the napkin covering the shot glass. To everyone's utter amazement, the quarter has disappeared. Be sure to whisk away your materials lest your trick's secret be revealed.

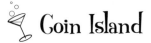

Coin Island

PROPS: Matchbook, 6 quarters, ashtray, highball glass, water

GOAL: Free drinks

Pour about a quarter inch of water into the ashtray. Bet your friends that you can move the water out of the ashtray without moving the ashtray. Stack the quarters in the center of the ashtray so the top two quarters are above the water. Place four unlit matches on top of the quarters. Light the matches and immediately cover the flame and quarters with the glass. The water will be drawn into the glass. Drink up, matey!

Dollar-Bill Beer

PROPS: Empty beer bottle, crisp dollar bill

GOAL: To make a buck

Ask a friend for a crisp dollar bill. Turn an empty bottle upside down on top of the dollar. Bet your buds you can get the dollar out from under the bottle without knocking over or touching the bottle. Their murmurs will soon turn to amazement as they watch you do just that. Simply roll up the dollar until it pushes off the bottle. Then pocket the dollar. If you're with wealthy friends, ask for a fiver!

 Egg Float

PROPS: Glass of water, egg, salt shaker
GOAL: To make an egg float

Take a glass of water and carefully drop an
egg into it. After the egg sinks to the bottom
of the glass, bet your buddy a free drink that
you can make the egg float. After she rises to
the challenge, shake some salt into the glass,
stir, and watch the egg rise to the surface.
You've just earned yourself another Gimlet!

The Bar Balance

PROPS: 3 empty highball glasses
GOAL: To balance three identical glasses on
top of one another

This is a good follow-up to other bar tricks
involving balance. Once you have enraptured
your audience with other feats of magic and
wonder, tell them you can balance three identical
glasses without any visible means of support.
Keep the face of a clock in your mind's eye while
you perform this trick. Place the first glass on the
bar. Place the second glass on top of the first
glass in the ten o'clock position. Place the third
glass on top of the second glass in the two o'clock
position. There you go!

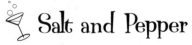 Salt and Pepper

PROPS: Salt, pepper, small plastic comb

GOAL: Free drink, as always!!

Make a small hill of salt, about the size of a
quarter, on the bar. Sprinkle a small amount of
pepper on top of the salt. Bet your friend a drink
that she cannot get the pepper off the salt without
disturbing the salt. Of course she can't, but you
can. Take your plastic comb and comb your hair
a few times. Then hold the comb over the salt
and pepper. The static electricity will lift the
pepper off the salt.

Indexes

By Author and Source

By First Line

When you depart from me, 45

When you meet someone better than yourself, 88

When you understand one thing through and through, 107

When you're sitting at home with nothing to do, 189

Whenever a man's friends begin to compliment him about looking young, 17

Whenever they rebuild an old building, 159

Where liberty dwells, there is my country, 166

Where'er you walk, cool gales shall fan the glade, 32

Wherever your life ends, it is all there, 14

Who can deceive a lover?, 141

Who ever loved, that loved not at first sight?, 140

Who fed me from her gentle breast, 152

Who'd care to be a bee and sip sweet honey from the flower's lip, 60

Whoever knows thyself, 157

Whoever rescues a single life, 177

Whom the gods love dies young, 103

Whoso findeth a wife findeth a good thing, 208

Whoso has done an atom's weight of good shall see it, 42

Whosoever surrenders his face to God and performs good deeds, 42

Why did she love him?, 147

Wine brings to light the hidden secrets of the soul, 69

Wine improves with age, 71

Wine is a mocker, 64

Wine is good as life to a man, 66

With God I have no fears, 36

Without money, honor is no more than a disease, 217

Wives are a young men's mistresses, 129

Wives in their husbands' absences grow subtler, 209

Woman: the fairest work of the Great Author, 132

Women, you can't live with 'em, 132

Women are made to be loved, 131

Women were ever things of many changing moods, 131

Work banishes those three great evils, 218

Work is good, 222

You are never too old to set another goal, 26

You can always read a doctor's bill, 177

You can do anything in this world if you are prepared to take the consequences, 4

You cannot run with the hare and hunt with the hounds, 107

You foam within our glasses, 62

You gave us life, 82

You have become mine forever, 205

You may give them your love but not your thoughts, 31

You never find people laboring to convince you that you may live very happily upon a plentiful fortune, 220

You pays your money and you takes your choice, 216

Young men think old men fools, 26

Your absence has gone through me, 46

Your cup, 135

Your diamonds are not in far distant mountains or in yonder seas, 106

Your family will always be your home, 78

You're never going to get anywhere if you think you're already there, 190

You're never too old to become younger, 25

You're not too old when your hair turns gray, 26

Youth is a blunder, 24

Youth knows no age, 21

Youth that rides the wildest horse, 56